Rishi Ram Ram

Yogi M.K. Spencer

UNDERSTANDING THE DIVINE MYSTERIES

By

H.S. Spencer

and

Yogi M.K. Spencer

Edited by

Dr. S.P. Ruhela

Regency Publications

New Delhi 110008

ISBN 81-86030-71-9

Published by Regency Publications, 20/36-G, Old Market, West Patel Nagar, New Delhi 110 008 and printed at Radiant Printers, New Delhi, Phones: 574 0038, 571 2539; Telefax: 578 3571.

Editor's Note

This book *"Understanding the Divine Mysteries"* is a combined publication of two great spiritualists's works — Homi S. Spencer's book *'The Mysteries of God in the Universe'* and his cousin brother Yogi Minocher K. Spencer's book *'Divine Discourses & Poems'* both of which had been initially published by the then Spiritual Healing Centre, Coimbatore over fifty years back. They were widely appreciated by enlightened readers and the press because of their spiritually enlightening and uplifting contents and beauty of their style.

Since the closure of the Spiritual Healing Centre in 1965 and the death of these two great spiritualists these books have remained out of print for long. Sri K.S.D. Aiyer, Secretary of the Spiriual Healing Centre, as copyright holder for these books had authorised Sri A. Somasundaram, Divine Centre, Markapur (A.P.) to get them published, and the latter in turn has authorised me to get them published after due editing.

I have pleasure in being associated with these valuable books as editor and in getting them published on behalf of the Sai Divine Research Centre, Faridabad, which has been established by us as an extension of Sri A. Somasunderam's DIVINE CENTRE at Markapur — both these centres being involved in carrying forward the mission of the Spiritual Healing Centre to spread spiritual knowledge.

We express our gratitude to the great souls of H.S. Spencer and Yogi M.K. Spencer and K.S.D. Aiyer who had blazed the trail of spiritual awakening in India in the 1940s & 1950s under the benevolent guidance of the Spirit Master Rishi Ram Ram.. Grateful thanks are due to Swami Amritanandaji, Spirit Guide of the World presently, and Sri A. Somasunderamji.

It is earnestly believed and hoped that the readers will be immensely benefited by this beautiful book on spirituality. It will promote boundless optimism and strength to face the present world and the after world.

June 18, 1998

Prof. Satya Pal Ruhela
Professor of Education (Sociology)
Founder & Secretary
Sai Divine Research Centre
126, Sector 37, Faridabad 121 003

Foreword to M.K. Spencer's book 'Divine Discourses and Poems'

I am grateful to Sri Minocher K. Spencer for giving me this opportunity of serving the Lord in him and the blessed readers of this monumental work, by writing this short foreword to a book which bears the stamp of "revelation".

Even a cursory glance of the illuminating contents of this work is enough to convince the reader of the inspirational character of the sublime thoughts it conveys. A deeper study is bound to effect life-transformation. The author's direct, arresting style helps this process and takes every word directly into the heart of the reader and produces a lasting impression on his mind.

Only a *Siddha* can produce such a work. Only a Great Master's words can have such spiritual force. Every Discourse throws a flood of light on the *Sadhaka's* Path towards Self-realisation. Again and again the author has laid the greatest emphasis on selfless service and purity of heart and mind. He has declared in unequivocal language that God is to be realised through love of all beings, through service of all His children. Selfless service and cosmic love are the Ganga and the Home are worth memorising and singing in the morning. Write them on the tablet of your heart. You will hear the music of the Soul and be drowned in the ocean of bliss and peace.

Sri Spencer has rendered a distinct service to humanity by presenting in this work the very essence of real religion, the various Paths that lead to God, and the fundamentals of various religions. He has beautifully brought out the truth that all religions are fundamentally one. "Divine Discourses" is a timely publication which will unite the hearts of people following different religions, and which will stir up spiritual aspiration in the heart of every man and woman in the world. May it shed light on thy path!

May God bless Sri Spencer with health and long life in the service of humanity, peace, prosperity and Kaivalya Moksha

Ananda Kutir, All-Souls Day,
Ist November, 1951

Swami Sivananda
Chuihende Ashram
Shivanand Nagar
Rishikesh (UP)

Preface to 'The Mysteries of God in the Universe'

The Laws of God are so many mysteries to so many yet. The Laws of Reincarnation and Karma are a part and parcel of them. But none of these mysteries can be understood without understanding the Fundamental Principles of Spiritual Philosophy which lie at the root of them all. They are meant to explain the condition of LIFE both in the Visible and Invisible Worlds and thus help forward the Realisation of SELF and the SELF of all INDIVIDUAL SELVES. This little volume is therefore written as an humble effort to help understand such of the Mysteries of God as would help to understand the mysteries of Reincarnation and Karma which are a part and parcel of the teaching of the great Prophets of the great Monotheistic religion of the world today.

Enough positive evidence has accumulated so far in support of the facts of Reincarnation and Karma and it all goes to show the correctness of the underlying Fundamental Principles of Spiritual Philosophy. If this volume helps its readers to understand and realise the Real SELF within each and through the

INDIVIDUAL SELF to realise the ABOSULTE SPIRIT — the GOD WITHOUT — this humble effort will have been more than rewarded. May it be so by the Grace of God, is the humble prayer of the author.

May 6, 1957

Prof. H.S. Spencer

Contents

Editor's Note iii

Foreword to M.K. Spencer's book 'Divine Discourses and Poems v

Preface to 'The Mysteries of God in the Universe' vii

Part I: The Mysteries of God in the Universe

1. The Mysteries of God in the Universe 3
2. Conscience, Consciousness and the Soul 37
3. Where to Seek Proofs of Reincarnation 46

Part II: Divine Discourses on God, Nature and Life

1. God 59
2. The Blessed Ones of God 63
3. The Path of Asha 65
4. The Voice of Silence 70
5. Liberation from the Wheel of Birth and Death 73
6. Immortality 77
7. The Mystical "Seven" 80
8. The Two Choices 84
9. Birth and Death 87
10. The Four Paths 90
11. The Way to Salvation by Disinterested Action 95

12. The Path of Devotion 97
13. The Path of Wisdom 101
14. The Path of Meditation 106
15. God and *Maya* (Nature) 111
16. Spirit and Matter 116
17. The Light of Love 121
18. God and His Angels 126
19. Nature's Grandeur 130
20. Religion 134
21. Masters 138
22. One World Government and One World Religion 145

Part III: Spiritual Poems

1. Soul's Growth 153
2. God's Messenger 155
3. The Blind Begger 156
4. Nature's Beauty 157
5. God — Life's Goal 159
6. The Martyr 160
7. The Mystic 161
8. We want Brotherhood, not War 162
9. Reincarnation 163
10. Cycle of Births 164
11. Fire 165
12. The Lame Leper 166
13. The World is my Home 167
14. Full Life 168
15. God-realisation 169
16. Forget not the Goal 170
17. The Storm at Sea 172
18. What Boon, I Seek 174
19. Bliss 175
20. Christ in Slums 177

21. Salvation 178
22. Salutations be to Thee, O God 179
23. Nature's Song 181
24. Crucifixion of Christ 182

Prayer

"O God, we pray that we may be soon launched into a New Era of one World Religion, one World Polity, one World Civilisation, one World Humanity based on the foundations of equality and brotherhood, service and co-operation.

We pray that our scientists may now begin to study the inner worlds and give us the benefit of their researches. It is not only the union of all mankind that we seek, but the union of the whole universe, the discarnate co-operating with the incarnate spirits for the glory of Thy Kingdom. It is by means of universal love and prayers, that we shall build up a new kingdom of the spirit".

(Late) Yogi M.K. Spencer
Author of 'HOW I FOUND GOD'

PART I

THE MYSTERIES OF GOD IN THE UNIVERSE

(Homi S. Spencer)

"Realization of God or His worship does not in any way add to the prestige of God. It is for our own benefit. We get a right understanding of ourselves and of God. It gives a new turn to our outlook, and our ignorance departs after knowing God, and surrendering to His will. Thus we get rid of our worries. We refrain from adopting any ugly means to profit ourselves at the cost of others."

— (Late) H.B. Sawhney
New Delhi

Chapter 1

The Mysteries of God in the Universe

In the articles on Reincarnation in the Gathas, the Holy Bible and the Holy Koran, we have seen the sanctions for the belief and factual acknowledgment of the doctrines of Reincarnation and Karma in the four great monotheistic religions of the world viz., Zarathushtrianism, Judaism, Christianity and Islam. The prevalence of these doctrines in Hinduism and Buddhism is so well known that the fact requires no mention.

Zarathushtrianism, Judaism, Christianity and Islam agree that:

1. Man has to return to his Maker, the absolute Spirit or God from Whom he has come and with Whom alone he can find Life Everlasting, that is to say, Life without Death or Life with conquest over Death.

2. Man can accomplish this return only with perfected attributes, and

3. That the perfection of these attributes is attainable only by life on Earth for which repeated births are thus a dire necessity.

The doctrines of Reincarnation and Karma are thus the corollaries of the fact of Spiritual Evolution or Evolution of the Soul which is the cardinal teaching of all revealed religions.

Having found the cause of Reincarnation and Karma in the evolution of the soul and the Scriptural Sanctions for the doctrines, let us proceed a little further in our examination of the subject from the point of view of Spiritual Philosophy which is that body of Knowledge which deals with the Laws of Existence in the Invisible and visible worlds, and is designed to teach what Reality is and how it can be attained.

This philosophy is based upon a few simple fundamental principles or postulates viz.:

1. That the Absolute Spirit or God is the Uncreated, Invisible, Infinite Cause of all causes and is thus Omnipresent, Omniscient and Omnipotent.

2. As such the Invisible becomes the Real and the Manifest and to come from the Unmanifest, so that all creation is the Manifestation of the Absolute Spirit and is the product of His Thought resulting in His Word. He says "Be" and it is.

3. As such He is Immanent in all nature and in every living thing including man; and yet, as all Creation is only that part of Him which is in Motion or Vibrations, He transcends all His Creations and is Transcendental also.

4. As Motions and Vibrations can vary, His Manifestation in the Cosmos is by mean of different Planes of Matter — all Matter of whatever kind being only Spirit in Manifestation vibrating on different scales in different Planes.

5. The existence of these different planes of Matter necessitates the embodiment of the matter of all these planes in the constitution of Man and this explains the necessity and the existence of the invisible and visible bodies of Man corresponding to the different planes of matter viz., Spiritual, Manasic, Astral, Etheric and the gross physical. These different bodies in Man are necessary to enable him to respond to the different ranges of vibrations of these different planes.

6. Consciousness residing in the Divine Immanence which is in all Nature — in all things and living beings, including man — consequently pervades the Universe and becomes the cause of all changes and adaptions. These changes and adaptions constitute Evolution which is the method by which the Divine Immanence is unfolded resulting in the steady enlargement of Consciousness from the Mineral through the vegetable and animal kingdoms to the human kingdom. Human consciousness is still however subject to many limitations and its further enlargement therefore entails the removal of these limitations. Their removal depends upon man's own efforts, which can be considerably aided by help from the Invisible World when sought in the right way.

7. Freewill thus becomes the most precious gift of God to man as a potent Motive Force in human evolution at all stages of Existence both in the visible and invisible worlds.

Let us examine the fundamental principles a little more closely. Whatever the line of thought and inquiry pursued in any system of natural philosophy based upon the conclusions of modern Sciences, à point is sure to be reached beyond which it will be difficult to proceed and at which the postulation of a First Cause Uncreated and Infinite and itself the Cause of all Causes, becomes a necessity. Its Infinity implies and proves Its Omnipresence; and when to this Omnipresence we are obliged to attribute a Stupendous Intelligence or a Mighty Mind from our observation of Law, Order and Progress in all the most complicated and intricate workings of the Macrocosm as well as Microcosm as is done by some of the best scientific minds of the day excelling in all the different branches of Science, severally and individually, we are obliged to and justified in joining Omniscience to this Omnipresence. This Omniscient Mind means Omniscient Consciousness because Consciousness is the only real faculty of the Mind and all the other faculties of the Mind are merely functional which would be inoperative without Consciousness. Further it is now being increasingly recognised that Thought is a great Creative Force. Witness its application in Psycho-analysis and Psycho-Therapy, in Moral Philosophy and in the building up of character and potency for success in life in an earthly sense, and in the education of normal and abnormal children and criminals. The best and most astonishing of its successful applications is in Yogic practices and meditation. These are its present uses and applications by à creature of very limited capacities like puny man. What can then an Omniscient Omnipresence not do with it? Such an Omniscient Omnipresence is necessarily therefore All Powerful or Omnipotent.

Having thus established the truth of our first fundamental principle we can see that it follows naturally from it that whatever exists must necessarily exist in that Grand Omnipresence and that Omnipresence has necessarily to be Immanent in everything. It is thus Immanent, in all the huge starry Universes-we use the word 'Universes' advisedly in the plural-as well as in the tiniest atoms and even in the electronic and protonic components thereof. The electrons and protons are however centres or concentrations of energy of different masses; and as in the cosmic interstellar spaces between different Universes and within each Universe there are continuous electromagnetic fields. So in the minute spaces between the electrons and protons within an atom, there do exist electromagnetic fields. As these fields are not completely filled with electrons and protons the special gaps whether in atoms or universes have to be presumed to be full of some other kind of energy for purposes of a continuum required for the different radiational purposes. This Energy is another form of Ether. Thus Ether is the matrix in which alone all the different electronic and protonic combinations of physical matter can exist. But whatever the form or condition in which Ether exists whether electronic and protonic or any other, ether is only a kind of energy. All energy being nothing but a form of Motion and as all Motions can vary, all Energy remains transmutable. There is another character of Energy which Radiation emphasises and that is its prevalence in octaves. The peculiarity of these octaves is that while the notes in each octave are related in a special progression, those in succeeding octaves are the same in quality differing only in acuteness. The terms "notes" and "acuteness" (or "pitch") are derived from the science of sound, but they go with the term "Octave" which is used by scientists in connection with sound as well as radiation. The difference in acuteness is due merely to a higher frequency and there is a definite ratio in which this frequency increases with each higher octave.

Our universe thus is nothing but pure Energy, some of it "imprisoned in electrical bonds" and existing in the forms of electrons and protons and some in which the negative and positive electrical charges are neutralized and existing in the form of photons. There are still some portions of it which must be considered as existing in an unconcentrated form serving as a medium for the wave-vibrations of its concentrated forms of electrons, protons and photons. Just as these concentrated forms act as particles possessing vibratory motion, the unconcentrated continuum must be understood to possess the same characteristics and its particles to be acting in the same way in another medium, serving as a matrix to it in the same way as Ether serves as a matrix to the physical. And that it is so, is shown by the existence of Auric colours which belong to the still finer or higher kinds of matter known as Astral, Manasic and Spiritual. Auric colours can not possibly be Etheric Radiations. We know that the colours of the flowers are due to the interception of the rays of Light of different colours. That is why the colours of the flowers are seen in sunlight or by lamp light but fade away in darkness. They are also constant. Auric colours are not due to the interception of any Etheric Radiations. They can be seen by those able to perceive the invisible bodies of man, both in light and darkness; and these auric colours are not constant. They change under the varying influences of man's emotions and thought, and are caused by these emotions and thoughts. They therefore clearly belong to the worlds of astral and Manasic matter. The Astral plane of Existence is also called the plane of Emotions and Feelings because the matter of that plane is the first to be acted upon by our emotions and feelings. In the same way the Manasic or Mental plane is so called because the matter of that plane is the first to be acted upon by our thoughts. Spiritual Philosophy teaches that the matter of these planes are selfluminous and this is shown by the way they are affected and display different colours according to the nature and intensity of different feelings, emotions and thoughts. The different feelings, emotions and thoughts act by way of differences in vibrations and thus produce different auric colour effects.

Here we enter a realm where Science has not still penetrated, but which it may be said to have just touched the bounds of. Even at these boundaries, it has discovered the following facts:

1. that man possesses several invisible bodies;
2. that these invisible bodies display variegated colours;

3. that these colours are affected by man's emotions and thought and show marked changes under their varying influences;

4. that there are people who have lived both in the past and the present days and some of whom are still living, who were or are able to see these invisible bodies and their auric colours and the changes in them.

5. that man continues as a living entity after physical death consciously functioning in these invisible bodies.

6. that there are persons living on earth today who are also able to function consciously in one or more of these invisible bodies. This is popularly known as going into *Samadhi*.

These discoveries have been made in the course of experimentations in Spiritualism or in the course of the collection of data for spiritualistic purposes. These experimentations have been made over and over again under very rigid test conditions by men of intelligence and integrity in various walks of life, scientific and otherwise, and have given uniform results which leave no room for doubt. These results have been published in numerous books on Spiritualism which are easily available to the earnest reader. There is however some misconception in the popular mind regarding Samadhi and so we may dilate here a little upon it.

What is Samadhi? It is a state of trance and the most important feature of that state is the separation from the physical of the invisible inner parts of one's self. This separation may take place at any of the invisible levels, that is to say, either at the Astral or Manasic or Spiritual level.

The second important feature is that the person going into trance becomes dead to physical surroundings, that is to say, he becomes unconscious of and impervious to physical surrounding, impulses and stimuli. His consciousness is transferred for the time being to the planeastral, manasic or spiritual — at which the separation has taken place.

He, however, may or may not be able to bring down into physical consciousness the impressions of his experiences on any of these subtler and invisible planes. That will depend upon the working of channels of communication between his various invisible bodies *inter se* and also upon that of the channel of communication between the lowest of them and the organ of his physical consciousness viz., his brain. The working of these channels is explained at some length in the author's pamphlet on "Conscience, Consciousness and the Soul" which is therefore included as the next chapter.

The word *'Samadhi'* in the stricter sense should be used for the separation of the Soul from all its sheaths, but it is more generally and more loosely used for any state of trance leading to any of the invisible planes. This is mainly due to popular ignorance of the fact that the trance state may lead to the functioning of the consciousness on any of these invisible planes.

There is however a vital difference between the true state of Samadhi leading to the highest or Spiritual plane and the popular state of Samadhi which may lead even only to the Astral plane, or maybe, sometimes to the Manasic plane. In the true state of Samadhi, the soul casts of all its sheaths and escapes only in its own Spiritual vesture to the Spiritual Plane, which in the popular states of Samadhi, remains clothed with the sheath of the plane on which it is working consciously for the time being and other sheaths finer than that.

There is also another point of difference. When the Soul is working on any of the lower invisible planes —Astral or Manasic — it keeps a kind of contact with the body or bodies of the plane lower than that at which the separation has taken place. For instance, if the separation is at the Astral level — as it mostly is — the link between the astral body and the Etheric and physical bodies is kept up by what is called the Silver chord. There must similarly be another link between the Manasic body and the Astral body which comes into use when the separation is at the Manasic level. It is not known to the present writer what is the exact nature of this link or how it is called.

When the soul however is able to separate from all its sheaths, it has generally by that time reached a state of union with the Spirit or Atman which is the God within each of us, so that while the soul separates itself from all its sheaths and goes out to explore the Spiritual world or plane, the Spirit or Atman on account of its re-union with the Soul, is able to supply the Spiritual controlling or executive agency which is necessary to keep the different bodies — invisible and visible — and their myriad cells together as one entire unit.

This state of re-union between the soul or *Jiva* and the Spirit or *Atman* is popularly known as complete Self-Realization and is spoken of even as God Realization. But even this state has distinct stage. For instance, as soon as a soul becomes capable of functioning consciously on the higher Manasic plane, it necessarily becomes cognisant of the Atman and the person or individual may be said to have realized Self. But it does not mean that the re-union of the soul or Jiva with the Spirit or Atman has actually taken place. What is achieved is the first step to this re-union. The Soul has yet to learn to separate itself even from its highest Manasic sheath before it can be re-united with the Spirit or Atman. Similarly, even when it has learnt to re-unite with the Atman it has in a way won God Realisation Strictly speaking, it is only the beginning of God Realisation, because the soul is not completely merged in the God without. It has only acquired the capacity for this complete merger through its re-union with the Atman, and as a matter of fact complete re-union with the Atman is not possible so long as the soul continues in a living physical body, though for all practical purposes of conscious thought, speech and action the re-union may appear and may be complete in the sense that the soul thinks, speaks and act all the time only in accordance with the dictates and wishes of the Atman. Similarly in as much as the Atman is always in complete accord with the dictates and wishes of the God without or the Absolute Spirit pervading the universe, the soul may for all practical purposes be considered as God Realised.

In this discussion on Samadhi it will be found that we have found the key to the enlargement of human consciousness which has been spoken of in the sixth fundamental principle or postulate of Spiritual Philosophy noted above. This enlargement of Consciousness is through conscious functioning, in the different Invisible Planes of Existence in the different invisible bodies with which we are endowed. But for a proper conscious functioning what is required is a purification and strengthening of the vehicles through which the functioning has to take place. This is the object and purpose of the meditation and other practices involved in the different systems of Yoga viz., Bhakti, Karma, Gnan and Raj. Of these Bhakti Yoga is the simplest and safest and it is therefore that is enjoined in all Revealed Religions. It can be and should be practised by everybody. It can be practised during waking hours by setting apart a very small fraction of our waking hours period of sleep through dedication of our soul to the Service of others as God may direct, guide and control. This last may seem a very strange and bizarre idea but "Serve while you Sleep" is a literally true slogan and its technique is most simple. The only precedent conditions are (i) a real desire to serve others in ways God may find your soul fit for and (ii) no desire to know for what service or services God uses your soul and how He uses it.

Here we have the daily practice of *"Saroshem Mazdai"* or complete Faith in God and Complete Surrender and Obedience to His Will which is the essence of Bhakti Yoga, resulting in its fruition in the best and highest form of *Nishkama Karma* or Desireless Action. Such daily practice must slowly but surely transform any human being into a God-like entity by a double process of purifying and strengthening his invisible bodies. A stage will be reached in this process when this *Nishkama Karma* will begin to flower into. Gnan and the enlargement of Consciousness will begin to make itself felt even in the waking consciousness in various strange and mystifying ways. Even then Saroshem Mazdai must be practised also in that regard. The idea is to leave everything to God to make you a fitting instrument for the expression of HIs wishes and Self through yourself, so that His Will may easily reign supreme on Earth as it is in Heaven.

It may be asked: If we leave everything to God where does our Free Will come in and what is the good of it to us? The answer is very simple. The very act of leaving everything to God for the purpose of making one a fitting instrument for the expression of His Wishes and Self through one's Self, is in itself the highest and noblest act of the exercise of one free Will. Without the exercise of one's Free Will the act of complete faith in God and complete self-surrender to His Will is impossible and where this very first step in Spiritual progress is tabooed — again by the exercise of one's Free Will — all the subsequent progress is barred, and the limitations on one's Consciousness are made more rigid.

Even if the correct exercise of One's Free will does not free us from one's shackles during one's life on earth, it will not matter. The first step to freedom will have been taken and the impulse to the soul's freedom started on Earth will have been greatly strengthened by its continual daily practice and will continue stronger in post-mortem existence, so that, that freedom will still become possible even after Earth-life. But where the first step is not taken and the impulse not sustained and strengthened through daily practice, that impulse must reach a point even in post-mortem existence where it fails to stir to further action and progress for the emancipation of the soul, and the soul stagnates. The Soul being a particle of divinity and being of the same Essence as God must constantly aspire towards the Light, Freedom and Bliss of its original state of Existence and must therefore seek some way of freedom from this stagnation. It can understand and will be made to understand that his stagnation is due to its own lethargy during earth life. The Soul's awareness of the cause of its failure to achieve freedom will become acute. On the other hand, the conditions of its invisible vehicles will attract them to thoughts and desires of an order which can be easily expressed through them, and whose expression will be either easy or possible only in life on Earth. The combination of this inward Soul urge and push for perfection and purification for the freedom of Divine Existence and the acuteness of its awareness of the cause of its past failure or failures to achieve its freedom and the pull of thoughts and desires which can be best expressed in and satisfied through life in familiar circumstances on Earth, will and must bring the Soul to seek relief through incarnation in another tabernacle of flesh. Thus we see that the fundamental postulates or principles of Spiritual Philosophy enumerated above drive us to the conclusion of the inevitability of repeated re-births during the imperfect state of the divine attributes of our souls. Once these attributes are perfected the existence of the gross environment for their growth becomes unnecessary and the Soul gains it *Nirvana* i.e., freedom from the Cycle of Birth and Death.

There is another consideration which makes re-birth on Earth a necessity. Our Souls belong to a particular stellar system known as our Solar System. Though in post-mortem existence generally speaking the soul of an ordinary human being may be enjoying the freedom of intercourse with and travel to other stellar of Solar systems in the Universe to which our Solar System belongs for purposes of Evolution it is necessary that our Souls should find their habitat in our Solar System alone, and as life in gross physical bodies is possible in our Solar system on our Earth alone, it is easy to understand that we have to seek perfection of attributes by re-births only on our planet the Earth. The conditions of bodily existence on other planets belonging to our Solar System are different as we can learn from the physical condition of life thereon depicted for us by the Sciences of astronomy and astro physics and from what we are told about them as for instance in the Zarathushtrain Scriptures. In Hormazd Yasht (Yt. I) para 25, after pointing to Vohu Mano (or Saturn), Ashem Vahishtem (or Jupiter), Khshthrem Vayirim (or Mars) and Spenta Armaiti (or the Earth) and explaining to Holy Zarathushtra that they are His creations, Ahura Mazda goes on to say with regard to Haurvat and Amertat (or Venus and Mercury) that they are the 'Mizdem' i.e., returns or rewards to the Ashaunam or the pure who enter another order to existence, and that these are also His creations. The late Mr. Ardeshir Framji Khabardar in his monumental work in Gujrati called "New Light on the Gathas of Holy Zarathushtra" has very ably shown how the names of the Ameshaspentas are meant to indicate the names of the planets in our Solar System also and these identifications are taken from that book. It is significant how well the other named accords with the actual order of the planets in our Solar System beginning with the furthermost planet then known viz, Saturn.

It is clear from the para 25 of Hormazd Yasht that while the Ashaunam or the pure who enter another order of Existence i.e., who have passed out of the human order, may find their habitat on Venus or Mercury, the impure do not by inference and contradistinction pass out of the human order and have to remain in that order and cannot enjoy habitat on these two planets. They have to find their habitat by rebirth again on Earth which is described in the Gathas as "drujo-demano" or the abode of "Druj" or Evil.

The deductions from the fundamental principles of postulates of Spiritual philosophy not only make re-birth on Earth a dire necessity, but they also fully justify and uphold all the three Scriptural statements on which Zarathushtrianism, Judaism, Christianity and

Islam are agreed as the foundation on which their teaching of the Laws of Reincarnation and karma are based.

Never was a profounder truth declared than when Holy Jesus taught that we live and move and have our being in God. It is fully justified and proved by the very first postulate of Spiritual Philosophy. Since everything comes from God, the Absolute Spirit, Man or rather the permanent Spiritual parts of him which are known as the Spirit and the Soul also come from God, and being of the same essence as the Divinity have to evolve back to their original Spiritual state to gain Life Everlasting. This can only be done by shedding everything which keeps them away from their pristine state i.e., by shedding all limitations on perfection of their own inherent Divine Nature and this as we have seen can only be done by constant rebirths on Earth.

There will still be many who will not be satisfied with this kind of deductive reasoning. Most people in the West and many in the east who have come very strongly under the influence of Western education are so materialistically trained and educated, that they find it difficult to accept easily the Spiritual truths which to the equally logical but spiritual trained minds seem so simple and self-evident. The materialistically trained minds refuse to accept as truths what even the prophets of the very religions they profess to follow have declared as truths known personally to them and which they have declared as having been taught to them by God. These materialistically trained minds will accept only truths based on what they call positive evidence. For such if they are honestly prepared to take to trouble the present writer had suggested in 1952–53, three liness of investigation and research in his pamphlet "Where to seek Proofs of Reincarnation". For the sake of ready reference, that pamphlet is re-published herewith as Chapter 3.

The three lines of investigation suggested in that pamphlet are through hypnosis, mediumism and yogism. Out of these three satisfactory result have already been obtained through mediumism as can be seen from the Life Readings given by Edgar Cayce; and also through hypnosis as evidenced by the book *"Reincarnation - Fact or Fallacy?"* by Geoffrey Hodson, published by the Theosophical Publishing House, Adayar, Madras in 1956. At page 30 thereof Mr. Hodson says:

"While the only proof of the truth of the doctrine of reincarnation consists of direct knowledge of one's own past lives, convincing evidence is provided by Colonel de Rochas in his book 'Les Vies Successives'. Therein he describes experiments with various sensitives put into a trance state by hypnotism. By the process known as regression of memory, the operators succeeded in taking their subjects back to their former incarnations, thus obtaining details, often of a historical character, which when checked later, were found to be entirely correct."

Thus two lines of investigation and research suggested by the present writer have already proved fruitful and given very satisfactory results. Mr. Hodson opines "that the only proof of the truth of the doctrine of reincarnation consists of direct knowledge of one's own past lives" and that is also possible. It is by way of Yogis, the third line of investigation suggested by the present writer in the aforesaid pamphlet, practised by the investigator himself. There can be no system of Yogism which rules out meditation as the most important integral factor. As explained at pages xvii and xviii of the introduction to "Spiritual Flashes and Earthly Lights" published by the Spiritual Healing Centre, R.S. Puram, Coimbatore, S. India, in meditation practised as an Yogic Sadhana, the only subject permissible is the idea of God, and this kind of meditation has four distinct stages. Yogic meditation upon God expands the consciousness and therefore these four stages are marked by different stages of Consciousness and are known as" those of Intellectual Consciousness, Intuitional Consciousness, Super-Consciousness and Universal Consciousness **AT WILL**".

Yoga, literally means, 'becoming one with'. It comes from the root 'yug', 'to join'. It is a mistake to suppose that in practising meditation as a Yogic Sadhana i.e., to say as a means of ordinary life of an ordinary citizen or householder is necessary. The less the departure the better God does not want any of his children to remain in ignorance. He wants each and every one of them to know 'the Truth and He has therefore imposed very simple precedent conditions for the different ways in which he can be approached by His children-by each of them according to his predilections and opportunities in life. The only important condition precedent applicable to all the ways of approach, are sincerity of purpose, a real aspiration to learn and practise the truth, and an honest desire to surrender to His will in good faith. All these precedent conditions are within the capacity of every one of us to fulfil, while we live our ordinary lives as common householder.

It is a mistake to suppose that the practise of bodily austerities is a necessary preliminary. Physical fitness and well-being, if anything, are real aids to yogic practices. Neither austerities nor indulgence in harmful habit should therefore be allowed to destroy physical fitness and well being. Nor is it necessary to good and successful meditation to practise painful bodily postures while meditating. Bodily relaxation, if anything, is a good help to meditation, but this relaxation does not mean slothful, lethargic or impious and offensive postures. Sitting cross-legged in the ordinary way, but comfortably, not necessarily in the lotus — asana is quite enough. Let everything be done in a natural, simple and easy way. Meditation is an act or mental discipline. The mind is a subtle, agile illusive Pimpernel. Meditation is an attempt to train it into different ways of behaviour. Why should we create further unnecessary difficulties in our work by subjecting the body to painful postures when engaged with so subtle, agile and illusive an opponent? Sitting cross-legged on the ground on a piece of matting or carpet specially reserved for the purpose is quite enough and is preferable to sitting in the same way on broad bench or chair. The reason is that sitting on the ground we are more directly in touch with the magnetism of the Earth which is helpful as an energiser. Sitting on the ground is also preferable because thereby we avoid the tendency and inclination to slouch and find it easier to keep up a straight back which helps concentrating on the Ajna chakra (between the eye-brows) or even the Brahma Chakra on the crown of the head.

In the matter of this concentration also the present writer sees no necessity to spoil the eyes and for becoming cross-eyed by fixing the gaze on the tip of the nose, when the concentration on the Ajna chakra can be managed ever so much more easily by fixing one's attention on the point between the eye-brows from behind the bony skull. This is a very simple technique which everybody practises when in deep thought. It is not painful, does not spoil the eyes and is in fact the natural, simple and easy way of doing the thing.

The purpose of meditation is the enlargement of Consciousness. The Ajna Chakra is in the Manasic body and by concentrating upon it we avoid the over-excitation of the Chakras in the Astral body and exposing ourselves thereby to the risk of over-stimulating the state of our desires and feeling. Moreover, the Ajna Chakra is the seat of Shiva's Eye which is popularly known as the Third Eye, though as a matter of fact this Chakra is different from the Eye of Soul or Spirit which is really speaking the Third Eye. This Third Eye resides in the Soul and not in the Ajna Chakra. The functioning of this Chakra must not, therefore, be confounded with the functioning of the Third or Spiritual Eye. Further by concentrating upon the Manasic Ajna Chakra we are trying to activate the mind which in its essence is Consciousness. We are thus by this act of concentration trying to stimulate our consciousness to expansion.

The first stage of meditation has been described as that of Intellectual Consciousness. We all are working at this stage even in ordinary life, and what we do in meditation is simply to deepen and intensify this intellectual Consciousness of ours. But we soon come to a stage when we find that we can not go any further along this intellectual line. We therefore give up conscious effort along this line and wait to see if any impulses will come to us spontaneously either from our own Soul or from some outside source which would add anything to our knowledge or consciousness of divinity which, it must be remembered, is the object of our search. When such impulses begin to reach our physical consciousness we have reached the second stage of Intuitional Consciousness in our meditative efforts. The essential condition of this state is stillness of the mind. As this stillness increases with practice, the Intuitional impulses become stronger and more frequent and the power and scope of Intuitional Consciousness increases. Here we are coming into a subtle, invisible and involuntary and therefore unconscious contact with our Soul, and through the Soul with our Atma or Spirit. It is the beginning of Self Realisation.

To establish ourself in Self-Realisation we have now to try and make this contact with our Soul voluntary and conscious. In our further meditative efforts we invite our Soul to make itself the ever-present conscious guide, director and ruler of all our thoughts, words and acts all the twenty four hours of the day and patiently, await this manifestation of the Soul to our physical consciousness. This manifestation may take place at first through signs, symbols or pictures, but it must result eventually in direct communication through words. When this direct communication with the Soul is established, we can tap our hidden memories of past lives and profit by what has been called Regression of Memory.

There are further stages of Spiritual Development but we need not discuss them here as our object was to find out how we could reach the memory of past lives by our own efforts along Yogism, and we have achieved our purpose.

The next question is how to meditate upon God? Here also the simpler the technique the better the chances of success for the ordinary householder. Select any one Name of God according to your predilection, and go on repeating it to yourself *softly* the while you have fixed your attention upon Ajna Chakra; and allow yourself as if it were, to be wafted upon its vibrations, but *without effort*. This effortlessness will ensure the full play of the vibrations upon you, while any effort will set up other vibrations which will hinder the full play of the vibrations of the name of God upon you.

If you would understand the wonderful potency in any of the names of God, remember that a great criminal and murderer Valia Koli by name became the great Rishi Valmiki by repeating the word "Rama".

Another important point is not to expect any results. Here also Nishkama Karma or Desireless Action will help most. It is a common saying amongst Mahomedan fakirs that every step you take towards God, He takes seventeen steps towards you. Everyday when you meditae for a short while you are taking one step towards Him and you are taking another step towards Him every night if you adopt the technique of "Serve while you sleep". These two step of yours coupled with God's (17 plus 17) thirty-four steps towards you will automatically bring you thirtysix steps nearer God every day. You do not know what is the distance between you and God. It depends upon your past. You therefore can not know what time it will take you individually to bridge that distance. But you may be certain that you search for Him — and we must assume that it is sincere, — is surely bringing you nearer to Him every day. If it pleases God, He can any day cut short the distance and give you His Grace much before the time it would ordinarily fall due. This shortening of the distance and the time will be the measure of your sincerity in approaching Him.

A word to strong caution is necessary here. In the course of this process unfoldment of the Soul, and before the final stage is reached, the aspirant will be sorely tried and tempted into blind alleys by the sprouting of psychic faculties mostly connected with the Astral world. He has to be always vigilantly on his guard against the *voluntary use and development* of these faculties. These are known in Sanskrit as Siddhis and he who runs after them leaves God and runs to his own ruin. The aspirants' only objective is God and it should always remain God, even after Self or Soul Realisation. This is the *sine qua non* of all Spiritual Progress.

Having tabulated the propositions on which the Prophets of different monotheistic religions have based their teachings of the Laws of Reincarnation and Karma, having seen the truth of these propositions in the light of the fundamental principles or postulates of Spiritual Philosophy by deductive reasoning, having seen their truth also in the light of positive evidence supplied by three separate lines of investigation and research through mediumism, hypnosis and yogism, let us now consider some of the common objections met with in the course of discussions on the subject.

The first of these objections may be stated in the form that in the universal search for happiness, after the bitter experiences of misery and unhappiness all around, who would like to come back to earth life and more particularly under compulsion involving force or pressure from an external authority?

The reply to it is as under:

The Soul is a particle of Divinity and as such is of the same Essence as God. It therefore aspires towards the Light, Freedom and Bliss of its original Divine

State of Existence. During Earth life it finds its aspirations clogged by the limitations under which it lives. The Soul has to surmount these limitations to reach its original Divine State of Existence. They can be surmounted only by setting into motion the necessary progressive force and this is the object of the different systems of Yoga. But no system of Yoga can be pursued consistently without the exercise of the aspirant's Free Will. It requires Free Will not only to start the impulse towards Life Everlasting but also to sustain it all through Earth Life. The quality and strength of this impulse will determine the continuance, persistence and strength of the same impulse in post-mortem existence. Where the quality and strength of that impulse are weak. It must reach a point of exhaustion resulting in Soul stagnation. It is then that the Soul realises the cause of its failure to reach its desired end, This realisation on the one hand and the attraction towards unfulfilled thoughts and desires exercised upon it through the impure state of its Manasic and Astral bodies on the other hand, combine to induce the Soul to seek relief from its stagnant condition through reincarnation and life in familiar circumstances on earth, in spite of the bitterness of the experiences of life in a previous incarnation or incarnations. The awareness of the cause of its failure or failures deepens after every incarnation and adds to the Soul's zest to achieve success and surmount the limitations which fetter its progress to Freedom. Hence the urge or impulse to reincarnate, at times very quickly after death. Reincarnation can thus been seen to be an act of Free Will on the part of every Soul and not the result part of every Soul and not the result of compulsion involving force by an arbitrary external power. The Soul's impulse may be encouraged, nay may even be initiated and fostered by the Divine Will acting in that direction. God wants all His children to come back to Him as early as possible. But His ways are very subtle, and He gets every Soul to conform to His Will by an act to that Soul's own Free Will.

The second objection is that of fear of Transmigration into animal forms:

Humanity has travelled so far now in its Evolution that this fear is entirely false, being wholly imaginary. There is no basis left for it now, whatever basis it may have had in the very remote past in the history of human souls when they had just passed out of animal forms through the process of evolution.

The third objection that it involves separation of loved ones, precluding future reunion:

This is another unfounded fear based upon misconceptions. The first, misconception is as regards what survives and what re-unites. The really permanent and imperishable parts of our personality are the Soul and the Spirit. They are both of the Divine Essence and as such Everlasting. It is during the process of Involution that they have had to take up even the invisible bodies. These bodies as we have seen in the foregoing part of this essay in the discussion of Samadhi, have also to be given up to reach final emancipation. Once given up they disintegrate though slowly. The second misconception is to believe that love can be any mutual attraction as between any two bodies. Love is affinity of Souls, and because Souls are everlasting this affinity can last for ever, and there is no reason why two or more Souls joined together by soul-affinities cannot re-unite in the enjoyment of that affinity. It is because of this affinity that marriages are said to be made in Heaven. There is no other sense in which they are so made. It is possible that two souls possessing close affinity may not be re-united in physical bodies during any one incarnation. But their Soul afinity will always be there and will always be active though not known to the parties in their physical consciousness.

A fourth objection is: Why do we not remember our past lives?

In every new life we obtain a new physical body. Our physical brain in our new body carries no impressions of our former existence. These impressions live in the consciousness of our Souls and we have already discussed in a foregoing part of this essay how we can tap this hidden knowledge of the Soul by inducing what is known as regression of memory by practising meditation in the right way.

Another objection akin to the fourth is: Why are we made to suffer without knowing what we suffer for?

The question implies that our present suffering is the effect of some cause set in motion sometime in the past. God does not want us to suffer without knowing what this cause is. He has no wish to make us thus suffer in darkness and He has actually provided us with the means of finding the necessary enlightenment. It is only our ignorance of this means which makes us suffer in darkness and in our ignorance we blame God for the want of this enlightenment.

The means is within us. It is in the accumulated essence of our past experiences which resides in our Soul Consciousness. This accumulate treasure is tapable by means of Yogic meditation which we have spoken of above.

Apart from this method of Self-knowledge this accumulated treasure is also tapable through the science of astrology. In fact as a professor of astrology has put it to the present writer: "The 400,000 sutras of astrological literature merely catalogue the consequences of Karma in its various manifestations which we crudely interpret as planetary influences"; so that "Astrology or Hora Sastra reveals the result of our past karma".

That we are not using the Yogic method of Self-knowledge or the astrological method of second-hand knowledge to dispel the darkness of our ignorance of the real causes of our sufferings is not a thing for which we can blame God. We have to blame our own selves for it. We fall ill and we do not blame the doctor for our illness. We go to the doctor for a cure but some diseases he is unable to cure. Still we do not blame the doctor. Similarly some of our Karma may be retrievable through the means prescribed in Mantra Sastra. Other parts of our Karma may be irretrievable though even here Mantra Sastra may be used not for changing but for minimizing the Karmic consequences.

We are the cause or originators of our Karma — whether retrievable or irretrievable — and we can not blame our Karma upon God. In both cases we ourselves in our ignorance or even after knowing what results will follow, have started the causes and all causes tend to run to their natural effects which we have to reap as consequences.

But even here there is a bright lining to the cloud. The way we react to the forces of Karma determines our future state. Take them in the right spirit and they cease to trouble both in the present and in the future.

There is still another very serious objection viz, that Reincarnation ignores the law of heredity.

In the first place it is not right to say that the Law of Reincarnation ignores or even denies the Law of Heredity. It acknowledge the Law of Heredity and makes use of it for its own purpose of Soul evolution. The Soul inhabits a body and in the selection of that body, apart from considerations of Karmic ties, the kind of body it will inherit frim the would be progenitors of the physical vehicle in which it is to be encased afresh, must become an important consideration for the soul seeking re-incarnation in flesh.

Secondly, assuming for a moment that there was nothing like the Laws of Reincarnation and Karma and that the laws of Heredity alone governed the whole case from beginning to end, would the latter enable us to explain all those variations and differences in mental, moral and physical qualities and characteristics which are easily explained by the physical qualities and characteristics which are easily explained by the Laws of Reincarnation and Karma — differences noticeable not only between man and man qua man, but also between children of the same parents and members of the same family? Clearly not and therefore the Laws of Heredity can not replace the Laws of reincarnation and karma. Both have their respective spheres of work and influence and both are complementary to each other.

Prof. V.H. Mottram in his book on *The Physical Basis of Personality* (Pelican Books, p. 139) after discussing in good detail genes, glands, chromosomes as the physical causes of personality, asks: "Is there no hope of our getting into touch with what is behind the sense perceptions upon which our 'knowledge' of 'matter' depends?" (page 137). In reply to this question he turn to a 'special kind of non-rational experience' of the mystics, and explains' that "they receive immediate assurance of the existence of a Something, a Unity., behind the data of the senses, which is as real to them as their as their own existence. I know, for instance, that 'I am much more certainly than I know that the pen with which I am writing these words 'is'. I know of the existence of the pen only through the sense impressions I obtain from it. But I need no sensory approaches to tell me that I am. The truth of my existence is much more immediate to me than the truth of the existence of my pen" (Page 137)

"...Now the knowledge which the mystics claim has that same immediacy as my knowledge that I am. The mystic does not feel, he knows." (page 138)

After discussing the experiences of various mystics and mystical writers as if it were in refutation of the well-known plea that all mystical experiences are pathological in origin, and emphasizing the "extraordinary fundamental likeness" of all accounts of mystical experiences. Prof. Mottram finally suggests that "the real 'I', the core of our being that thing so alien from the everyday 'I', is a spark, an atom of the fundamental Reality in the Universe, but that its activities are conditioned, moulded and determined by inheritance and nurture. A person is thrust upon it by our genes and our upbringing." (page 147.)

This 'persona' is a mask as shown by its root meaning such as used to be worn by actors. How truly has Shakespare said: "All the world's a stage and men and women only actors."

All the same 'it is a common place", as Prof. Mottram says (page 147) "that the core of one's being is often at war with the cupidities and desires, the whims and fancies of the normal self. Man is divided against himself, and only becomes whole when the inner core is integrated with the outer more personal self, when the everyday 'I' becomes one with the inner 'I'". It is this integration which the Laws of Reincarnations and Karma seek to achieve through the Laws of Heredity.

There is yet one more objection to Reincarnation which is quite as serious as the last. It is to the effect that there should be no necessity for a return to Earth life and that the Soul can progress on its journey to its Maker even in the Invisible Planes.

There is no necessity to deny the Soul's progress in the Invisible Planes. But it must be remembered that there are limitations to this progress. The Soul can not progress beyond the limits of the plane or sub-plane to which the state of its invisible vehicles permits as shown by its aura. It has woven the textures of these vehicles by it thoughts and desires in Earth life and those textures can not be completely changed during its post-mortem existence, except it be by a purifying and strengthening force started in Earth life. It is the quality and vitality of that force which decides what further progress the Soul can attain in its post-mortem existence. If that force is strong enough completely to overcome the strength of other forces brought into post-mortem existence from its Earth life and which pull in other directions, there will be a chance for the Soul to gain its Nirvana or freedom from the Cycle of Birth and Death during its existence upon the Invisible Planes after death. But if the requisite strength be wanting in that uplifting force, it will be a case of a resultant of forces and the uplifting force will at one time or another have spent, its strength. Its effect will then be neutralized by other forces and the stagnation of the Soul which has been spoken of in the foregoing part of this essay, will ensure. After that it is a question of time only before the Soul again elects to seek fresh incarceration in flesh on earth in the pursuit of its ultimate aim of

Complete Emancipation and return to its pristine state of Light, freedom and Bliss in the Ocean of Divinity.

Belonging as it does to our Solar System there is no choice for it but to find incarnation in flesh on our planet only.

Chapter 2

Conscience, Consciousness and the Soul

Man is a bundle of various moral qualities, some good, some bad and of different degrees of intensity. In his response to any of them it will be observed-and the manner of his response is an observable fact — that his reaction in some cases is almost instinctive and instantaneous, while in others it is not so. Why this difference? It is because the experience of that particular quality which he has gained through former lives, has sunk into his consciousness in all its quintessence. That particular quality — whether good or bad — has become fixed in his character and personality. His reaction therefore has become spontaneous, instinctive and instantaneous.

If it is a good quality it has become one with his conscience and a part of his enlarged spiritual consciousness. If it is a bad quality, it has so completely smothered his conscience that his spiritual consciousness has ceased to have any say at all in the matter, and it is only after he has tasted the bitter fruits of his actions prompted by that bad quality and drunk deep the cup of remorse, that in some future life he will find the hold of that quality weakening over his personality. His conscience in that future life will begin to be heard with regard to his actions based upon and prompted by that quality. It may be that even then the voice of his conscience in that regard may be so feeble that he may continue to disregard it. He will then require another birth or some more births, before that voice becomes strong enough to help him to gain control over that quality till at last after repeated mistakes, that quality is completely smothered in its turn and his spiritual consciousness has gained a victory over it.

Conscience and Spiritual consciousness are thus seen to be closely allied. Conscience or 'DAENA' is a part of Spiritual Consciousness or 'CHISTI'. It is that part of it which has sunk into and become a part of his personality; and in as much as Spiritual Consciousness is wholly good and divine, conscience must be taken as the part of Spiritual Consciousness which has become fixed in a man's personality as a good quality. A bad quality which has become fixed in his personality is also therefore the result of the absence of the Spiritual Consciousness working in him in that behalf.

Mind in the ultimate analysis is only Consciousness and this consciousness resides in the soul which is the Spiritual part of man. That is one simple fact and another simple fact is that for man to be aware of anything i.e., to carry the impression of anything, this Consciousness has perforce to make use of a a physical organ viz., his brain. It is the brain which receives all impressions and makes man aware of them —

whether these impressions come from the objective or subjective world.

Objective impressions as they are to be here understood, are those which come from sources external to man, even though they may come from invisible worlds; so that as regards these objective impressions, we have to consider separately those that come from the visible world and those that come from the invisible worlds.

Impressions from the visible world are sense impressions which are carried to the brain through our nerve organisations. The question then arises — do these impressions stop with reaching the brain, or are they also conveyed to the soul before they are reflected back by the brain into physical consciousness?

It is worth noting that the brain does not reflect back into physical consciousness all the impressions which it receives though the different senses at any one given moment of time. There are many things which we see simultaneously all of them do not enter our physical consciousness though all the impressions are registered automatically by the brain. It is the same with hearing and the other different sense faculties. This shows that there is some discriminating and controlling agency which may or may not allow the reflecting back of these impression received by the brain.

Is this control also exercised by the brain or is it exercised externally to the brain? And if the latter, what is this other controlling agency? The obvious reply is that this controlling agency is not the brain itself and this is best proved by illustrations.

When a person is, say, running along a road intent upon fetching, say, a doctor for some very near and dear one whom he has left seriously ill in his house, and happens to hear a loud report, say, as of two cars colliding, does he mind that report? No. Why? Because his mind is engaged upon a special mission and his Will not allow him to be side-tracked from that mission. When engaged upon such a special mission, it has been very often experienced that though he may see somebody well-known to him passing on the road, he will not be able to recognise him. Again his Will not allow him to be side-tracked from his mission.

Or again, say, a person in engaged in reading a book in which he is very much interested. It is a common experience that he is then unable to keep count of time, even though when he begin reading it, he has said to himself that he must close the book and go out to keep and appointment at a certain hour and there is a striking clock in the room where he is reading and the clock strikes the appointed hour. He hears these strikes but they they are unable to affect his physical consciousness.

All these examples show that the brain by itself is unable to reflect back the impressions received by it through the senses into physical consciousness without the guidance or behest of something else. In the examples we have examined we have denoted this something else as the Will in man. The examples also show that this Will is not a thing which exists by itself. It exists only as an attribute of the person and in some part of his constitution.

A man is constituted of (1) the Spirit, (2) the Soul, (3) the invisible bodies and (4) the physical body.

The *Spirit* is a particle of *Divinity* and is individualised but still forms part of the Ocean of Divinity and as such can be described as "universal". The whole of this individualised particle of Divinity however does not descend into an individual human being, but only a portion of it does. The portion which does not descend is the first constituent in man and is called his Spirit, and may be described as "a mere witness". It rules the Soul as its God.

The portion of the individualised Divine particle which descends is called the Soul. It is the second constituent of man. Coming from a Divine particle it is "an emanation from God". This emanation has necessarily all the qualities, nature and essence of Spirit, because nothing but Spirit or the Divinity can take on the first or Spiritual sheath. Becoming sheathed it also becomes individualised. It then takes on further sheaths viz., the invisible Manasic, Astral and Etheric bodies and the visible physical body. It remains clothed with the invisible bodies (not always all) and remains a 'Soul' till it has finished it rounds of experiences, becomes perfected and gets merged again into THE ORIGINAL DIVINE INDIVIDUALISED SPARK OR PARTICLE from which it started its career. While it has still to remain and function in its sheaths — all or less than all — it naturally acts as "the exercising body".

When we speak of the Spirit not descending but only the Soul doing so, the reference must be understood to be to descent in the sheaths lower than the Spiritual.

The process of the individualised Divine Particle's descent into man is the same — but of course, on a very miniature scale — as that of the descent of the Paramatma or the Cosmic Spirit into Cosmic Manifestation, involving Transcedence and Immanence.

Such is the constitution of man and in as much as all the bodies — whether invisible or visible — can be dropped by the Soul at some time or other, it follows that such abstract qualities or faculties as consciousness and Will, possessed by man, must necessarily abide only in the permanent. Spiritual part of him, viz., the Soul, if they are not to evanesce with the bodies when they disintegrate as they may at some time or another. Though the Soul and the Spirit are both permanent and Spiritual in as much as the Soul is the 'exercising body', we are constrained to say that these faculties abide in the Soul.

These attributes or faculties of the Soul can come into operation only at its bidding because they are not independent of it; and therefore to revert to our question, we may say that the controlling of the brain by the Will in man is in reality controlling by the Soul to which the Will belongs.

This being so, we may now go back to a previous question viz., are the objective impressions also conveyed to the Soul before they are reflected back by the brain into physical consciousness? The obvious answer is, it must be so — otherwise how can the soul act as the discriminating and controlling authority over the brain, allowing it to reflect back into physical consciousness, only some of the objective impression received by it and not other?

This raises a further question viz., how are these objective impressions also conveyed to the soul? The nervous organisations which receive the sense impressions from the visible world, by the vibratory undulations set up in them by these impression, create corresponding undulations traveling through these invisible bodies finally reach the Soul which is encased in them. The Soul then immediately sends back it instructions to the physical brain through the same channels in the invisible bodies of man by the same means of vibratory undulations. There is thus a constant process of action and interaction going on through the mechanism of the invisible bodies of man. It is practically the same as what takes place between the brain and the other physical organs of man through the affluent and effluent sets of nerves. The only difference is that the channels corresponding to these sets of nerves are in the invisible bodies and not in the visible physical body of man.

Coming now to the objective impressions coming to man from the Astral and Manasic invisible worlds, it may be noted that they are first received by the Chakras (or vortices) in the corresponding invisible bodies of man. These Chakras are the windows of the Soul for sending out to as well as receiving from the corresponding invisible worlds all messages pertaining to them. Once these messages are received by the respective invisible body, the process of sending them first upto the Soul and then again down to the brain is the same as described for sense impressions from the visible physical world. In trasmitting the message from the invisible bodies to the physical brain, the vibratory undulations of the Chakras first act upon their corresponding nerve plexuses from which the messages are conveyed to the brain.

In the course of their infiltration through the Manasic and Astral vehicles to the physical body and its organ, the brain, these impulses or impressions from the Soul are affected — and may sometimes even be distorted — by the conditions prevailing in the Manasic and Astral vehicles. The purer and stronger the states of these invisible vehicles, the clearer is the message of the Soul received by the physical brain. Otherwise the *'vrittis'* or whirlpools in these vehicles distort the message. Likewise a fuddled or muddled condition of the physical brain can also distort it.

There are also subjective impulses or impressions received by the brain. These are internal and come from the Soul and the process of their transference to the physical consciousness and the conditions which make for their successful or unsuccessful transference are the same as we have just completed noticing for objective impressions which are external to man.

Where the Soul is highly evolved and is able to function in its native land of the Spiritual Plane, the nature of cognisance is necessarily different, being by direct perception of the Reality, and where that Spiritual Perception is capable of and is allowed to infiltrate through the lower invisible planes on to the physical brain, without distortion, even the physical consciousness is pure and gets a true impress of the

Reality as it is, as in the case of Self and God Realised persons.

But so long as the Soul is enveloped in its shrouds, it cannot reach out to the Reality of the Spirit. It can reach out only to the reflection of Reality in the Manasic Plane, or to the reflection of that reflection in the Astral, or to the reflection of that Secondary reflection in the physical. That is why man's perception goes on changing till he realises God and also why it is necessary constantly to bear in mind that in the ultimate Reality everything is Spirit.

Chapter 3

Where to Seek Proofs of Reincarnation

Reincarnation today is not accepted as a scientifically proven fact though it is or may be, the best possible explanation of all the mental, moral and economic inequalities and differences noticeable between individuals. And yet it is possible to put the theory to test and prove it scientifically in various ways, in all of which Psychical Research Societies and in some of which psycho-analysis can take an important and decisive part.

The first of such ways is by means of the hypnotic trance. Once a person under the influence of hypnosis becomes objectively unconscious, it should be possible to reach his subjective consciousness, or his sub-conscious mind which, according to the theory of Reincarnation, is said to be brought with him from past incarnations and which is the storehouse of all his past experiences. This subjective consciousness ought therefore to be aware of that person's past births and so, details about such birth may be gathered for a large number of cases and if they are verified by subsequent search according to the directions obtained during the hypnosis, there would not remain any doubt as to the truth of such previous births. In this way the question can be settled once for all. Here is work for Psychical Research Societies and psycho-analysis.

This line of research is suggested by the part played by hypnosis in the early history of psycho-analysis and psycho-therapy. The development of psycho-analysis and therapy started with experiments in hypnosis, as shown by Geraldine Coaster in Ch. V of her book *"Yoga and Western Psychology."* At page 52 she says: "these experiments had taken the first step towards demonstrating the reality of the unconscious mind, the basic conception on which all analytical therapy depends."

Hypnosis was used by Charcot and Janet for the cure of physical diseases and its use was later extended by Freud and others to the diagnosing and elimination of mental disorders. It is true that in as much as cures by hypnosis were found to be uncertain and often only temporary, Freud subsequently elaborated a "skilled technique" for reaching the sub-conscious mind of his patients while fully awake, and thus ensuring a permanent cure which "was dependent on the full linking up of the two states of consciousness" viz., the waking and the dormant or the objective and the subjective.

The suggestion made here about using hypnosis as a means of reaching the sub-conscious for the sake of ascertaining the past experiences of the Ego in its former incarnations is therefore a possible and useful extension of the same method as was at first employed for the cure of physical ills and then of mental troubles. The method however is open to the serious objection that is may be put to undesirable selfish ends by uncrupulous investigators. If this can be effectively safeguarded against, there are many great possibilities existent in it of not only ascertaining incontrovertible evidence of the fact of reincarnation, but also of very important data for the all-round development and happiness of the individual whose sub-conscious is so contacted.

It may be argued that Freud's technique now obviates this danger but the danger of the unscrupulous use of the revelations even so received, still remains. There is also the further possibility that Freud's method may not after all succeed on account of the active operation of the individual will, which would be inoperative in hypnosis.

The most effective safeguard against the danger of the unscrupulous use of hypnosis and its results or that of the Freudian technique and its result, would seem to be to limit the use of either only to accepted Psychical Research Institutes of repute and expert psycho-analysts of repute. Any improper use of the result of the working of these institutes and practitioners of repute can also be further guarded against by strictly enforced rules of secrecy, and limitation of communication and publicity.

A variation upon this line of research would be the use mediumism in place of hypnotic trance. The form of mediumism may be either automatic or planchette or ouija board writing, or any one of the forms of trance mediumship. But here the difficulty is that the Guides on the other side may or may not consent to reveal the secrets about the previous incarnations of the sitter even though they voluntarily ask for the information in their proper person. Some Guides and communicators from the other side may even not be able to do so for want of access to the proper Akashic Records. Some of them however only may do so and that too in some cases only.

Even if the details in such cases can not be verified by subsequent search it should not matter. These details can be verified astrologically and if the results obtained *independently* from both these lines of research viz., through mediumism and astrology tally, they may not constitute what we may call a strictly scientifically demonstrable proof, but they would still be good logical proofs, and quite reliable ones for all practical purposes. What has been said here of the combination of the results of mediumism and astrology obtained *independently*, would apply equally well to the combination of the results of hypnosis or the Freudian technique and astrology also obtained independently.

The question therefore now is, can astrology supply any such fact about our past incarnations? The reply may seem very strange to many but it is in the affirmative. "Astrology or Hora Sastra reveals the result of our past Karma" says Prof. B.V. Raman at page 15 of his" Astrology and Modern Thought" and he say again at page 23: "planets therefore simply indicate the results of previous Karma". Hence the most important and primary part of astrological readings should be *to explain the nature and consequences of action done in past lives,* the effects of which have yet to run to fruition and then to explain whether these effects can be counteracted, and if so, at what stage and in what way, or whether these effects *will run their full course willy-nilly*. In other words, astrological readings should be reading of past karmas and explain how far these Karmas are retrievable or irretrievable, and if retrievable at what stage or stages and in what ways.

Now ordinarily astrological readings scarcely ever do this. They simply try to foretell what the stars are said to indicate. To that extent, they are unscientific, empirical and arbitrary, and encourage the belief in fate or destiny, and weaken the will power.

It is fully conceded that the fault is not that of the art or science of astrology, but wholly that of its empirical practitioners. The present writer knows of cases of friends — come of whom are still alive while others have passed beyond the Bar who have been fortunate enough to meet with astrologer who had in their possession astrological charts or Kundlies drawn on some kind of leaves or on copper plates which were related to one another, so that looking at the birth Kundlies of these friends, these astrologers simply found out other Kundlies in their possession related to these birth Kundlies, and read out to these friends what was written alongside these Kundlies and which writings explained the details of their present lives from their births onwards, in terms of their actions and other incident in their past lives. Here are Karmic relationship and sequence explained. But even these astrologers were only fortunate in having with them these ancient Kundlies. Without them they too would have been as empirical as many others, because the important point is to use the present set of planetary relations as revealed by a birth Kundli to find out what actions and influences of the past brought about the present set., There can be no effect without a cause.

The question then arises, it it possible to correlate the present set of planetary relation to any actions and influences in the past? Prof. Raman in a letter to the present writer dated 18-12-47 says: "The astrologer would simply read the past. In a work entitled *Karma Vipaka*, the question is elaborated in a masterly way, "... a careful study of a particular house in a horoscope reveals the nature of the actions done in past lives." In the same letter he says further on; "The 400,000 sutras of astrological literature merely catalogue the consequences of Karma in its various manifestations which we crudely interpret as planetary influences". The thing has been done. The result are ready to hand in these 4,00,000 sutras. But the rationale of the whole question still remains to be inquired into. The present writer is conscious of his own want of qualifications to enlarge upon so deep a subject and so requests others better qualified than himself to make it easy for others to understand and grasp the principles underlying it.

If the *sole real purpose of life* is so to evolve as to reach and become one with the Source of all Life, then all branches of knowledge, all sciences, should be made and utilised to subserve *that great purpose*; and Astrology as the science which shows the stage of development or progress reached in the fulfillment of *that great purpose* should explain the ways and means whereby that purpose may be best accelerated in the present span of life, and how that present acceleration can help further acceleration in the lives, if any, to be. In other words, it should be able to explain in terms of what is called *"Sanchita Karma"* the present or *Praradha Karma* and to guide how things can be mended to the individual's Atmic advantage.

"Sanchita Karma" *is the whole of the accumulated Karma of the past*, and Praradha Karma is *that part of it which a Jiva atma has come to pay off or experience the fruits of in the present incarnation*. This means that Sanchita Karma is much wider than the Prarabdha. According to the present writer's understanding of the Law of Karma, a Jiva Atma incarnates to pay off as many of its Karmic debts in any particular incarnation as it can. It is not ordinarily possible for it to pay off all its debts in one incarnation. But what may happen is that if it is fortunate enough to get proper Spiritual guidance, it tries to pay off many more debts than it came of events in the life of that Atma seems to run wide out of the Karmic orbit is due to what may be called Higher Spiritual Laws whose action is more compelling. Nor is it against the Law of Karma. In fact, it is very much the accentuated operation of the Law of Karma itself.

In this view of the Parabdha Karma it is implied that this Karma should necessarily consist for the most part of what is usually called bad or evil karma, the results of which however are equally necessarily modified by the good portion of the Sanchita Karma.

The karmic debt which one incarnates to pay off are therefore the resultant of the forces of evil and good Karmas of the past.

It also follows that the major portion of the good Sanchita Karma remains accumulated and necessarily so, because without such accumulation, spiritual progress and development of spiritual perfection would be impossible.

There is yet another line of research and investigation for ascertaining the proof of Reincarnation and it is connected with Yoga and Yogis. It is a line which is meant for Psychical Research Societies and not for psycho-analysts.

It is a well known fact that Yogis are able to look back into past lives — their own and those of others. They are able to do so because besides direct knowledge from direct contact with other Atmas, they are able to read what are known as Akashic Records with their Yogic vision. Even some psychic persons who are not Yogis are sometimes made aware of their past lives. This happens when they are shown astral or etheric pictures of events and incidents out of those lives, either in a waking state or in dreams. But this is different to the Yogi's direct knowledge from direct Atmic contacts and from Akashic Records. These are records preserved in the Manasic and Astral worlds, and we are told that they are very lasting — practically speaking, indestructible and more or less permanent.

Investigating parties from Psychical Research Societies can contact Yogis and try to collect from them fact as to the past lives of different persons who are willing to offer themselves as subjects of investigation, and then try to get these facts verified either actually and directly or if that be impossible by the indirect testimony of astrological readings as explained above. Even individual psychical research investigators can undertake the rigorous discipline of the different systems of Yoga and having reached the perfection of Yoga can verify out of their personal experience experience the truth about the powers of Yogis to look back into and read past lives.

Success in this Yogic method will entail a good Yogic development in the investigator; and as all true Yogic development depends primarily upon a good moral foundation, the danger of any unscrupulous use of the revelations brought out is very much reduced one might say almost obliterated. At the same time the possibility of wilful opposition from the subject under investigation is almost non-existent, because in such Yogic investigation besides the reading of the Akashic Records, the contact sought is purely Atmic and it is a condition precedent of such contact that the Atma condition precedent of such contact that the Atma of the subject under investigation is a willing partner in the operation. No Yogic Atma would ever force its decision or will upon any other Jiva Atma.

In the foregoing paras, three lines of investigation are suggested viz., through hypnosis, mediumism and yogism. Out of these three, satisfactory results have already been obtained through mediumism as can be seen from the following extract from an article on

Edgar Cayce, who died on 3rd January 1945 at the age of 67, appearing in the Magazine *Fate* for February 1953. It says:

"As Cayce went deeper into philosophical aspects of the work, he was able to give what he termed 'life reading'. He delved back into previous existences of the individual and learned the reason for that individual's present predicament. Often, armed with his knowledge the person could find the way out of present difficulties.

Frequently in these readings actual names and addresses of persons living hundreds of years ago were given as the previous incarnations of the subject of the reading. Even more astonishing was the fact that in every instance where this information was carefully checked against old records and historical documents, all data given was discovered to be accurate in every detail. Such persons had actually lived in the country, and town stated, in the year given and at the actual address of location mentioned.

Thus by combining clairvoyant medical diagnosis with life reading, Cayce was able to help many who could not be healed by medical treatment alone. Given an understanding of his past failing, the individual frequently was able to overcome that particular error which had resulted in despair, illness or tragedy in the present life."

(Cf. pages 106/107 of *Fate* for February 1953)

April 1953 —H.S. Spencer

PART II

DIVINE DISCOURSES ON GOD, NATURE AND LIFE

(Minocher K. Spencer)

DISCOURSE NO. I

God

God is the cause and seed of all creations in the universe, manifest and unmanifest. He is the Absolute Spirit that pervades throughout the universe. He is the Supreme Thinker the pivot round Whom the countless constellations in the Cosmos, move and have their being. He is the Soul of Souls. He is transcendent and immanent in nature. His breath is life. His word is Law. His power is immense. He is Eternal. He is Infinite. He is Omnipotent, Omnipresent, Omniscient. He is Love. He is Light. He brings joy in the universe with the light of His Love. He is Eternal Joy. He is *Sat Chit Ananda*. (Absolute Existence, Consciousness, Bliss). He is full of compassion. He hears every sorrowing soul, every repentant sinner. They have an asylum in His bosom. He does not discard them, when they pray to Him for mercy and forgiveness. He gives them courage and hope, the spirit of understanding and the power of endurance, to bear their fate heroically and manfully, for the Law of Karma is indispensable, irrevokable and irreducible. God's Justice is every tempered with mercy. He gives strength in the hour of trial and suffering.

God wants all His children to be happy, to put on the garment of contentment and not worry for tomorrow. Why cast shadows, when God is in every heart and every home. To live in God is to live in peace. To live in God is to love all, whether saint or sinner, wise or foolish, rich or poor.

To work for all is God's Law. Unselfishness is the crown of live. Selfishness is the thorn of live. God works for all. Motionless, He moves the whole universe in perfect unison and harmony. The sun does its work methodically and in perfect obedience to God's order, from day to day, without fault or default. It gives light and heat: it drives away sickness and sorrow from earth. It is a harbinger of Joy. It is a herald of God's majesty, His greatness, His glory, His power, his mercy, His compassion, His wisdom, His light, His love, His grace, His justice. The sun is the sustainer of life on the earth plane. If God were to withhold the sun from making its daily journey in the sky, from east to west, what would be our fate? We would be left in the slough of disease and darkness. Is it not then His great mercy, that He gives us sun's light and rays for the enrichment of our body and soul?

When the sun sets and the world is plunged in the quietness of the night, how beautifully is the sky studded with stars and planets, that emit their silvery light. And when the moon glides along the sky, as Queen of the Stars, how radiant we feel and what a thrill of joy and delight encompasses our heart, mind and soul?

Is not all this God's own glory? The sun and the moon, the stars and the planets speak of God's greatness and might. They are silent ambassadors of God's goodwill to all mankind. God's love to all human beings. God's grace and mercy to all His children.

And when we behold Nature — the majestic mountains, the valleys and ravines, the waves of the ocean roaring and moaning, the rivers rushing their way to the ocean, the tall forest trees, that stand like giants and defy the fury of the wind and storm, the green meadows, the rendezvous of that frolicsome deer and antelope, the humming bees, the chirping birds, the whistling wind, the fragrant flowers that delight the eye and the mind with their fragrance and lovely forms — are these not God's own creations for man's enthrallment and delight?

God is the architect of Nature. God is the object and target of every human being, whose soul progresses under God's Law of Evolution, from birth to birth, in every incarnation, till ripened with experiences and cleansed and purified, it seeks union with God, the Source of all Life. May God be every praised!

Might and Glory of God

O, let us sing of God's greatness and glory,
It makes a most enthralling story.
God was, is and will ever be
He pervades from mountain to sea.

To love Him is to adore Him.
To adore Him is to worship Him.
He alone is worthy of worship;
He alone is worthy of Kingship.

He is the monarch of our heart and soul.
He guides us to our goal.
He extends to us His loving hand;
He leads us to our life's end.

He is the seed, He is the fire.
He loves us in all attire.
His love is boundless.
His wisdom is endless.

He sent to us His prophet Zoroaster
The Great Magi, with a message to deliver,
The great message of Truth and Righteousness
And to love all in heart's fullness.

Krishna, Buddha followed him,
In those ancient ages, to our sight now dim.
Christ and Mohammad preached the same gospel.
They all our devotion impel.

Non-separateness is the aim of life.
Separateness is the seed of strife.
God is one, all religions are the same.
Let us pray together, man and dame.

Let us sing the praises of His glory
He is the Be-All in our life's story.
God is Love; God is Light
O, give us the inner sight.

DISCOURSE NO. II

The Blessed Ones of God

Who are the blessed ones of God? Those who seek God every minute of their lives in silent reverie of thought and in silent service of the poor and the helpless.

Those who work for God, like true soldiers in the battlefield, holding aloft the banner of righteousness, fighting their way against all ills of the flesh — lust and anger, greed and envy, pride and indolence.

Those who face adversity with a cheerful smile.

Those who harbour love for all, whether rich or poor, strong or weak, virtuous or vicious, saint or sinner.

Those who shun sin but not the sinner.

Those who walk with God, clothed in thoughts of God, pledged to serve all mankind without distinction of colour, caste or creed.

Those whose souls are in tune with the symphony of the wide universe.

Those whose minds soar into the lofty regions of divinity, though they are tied down physically to this earth plane of maya and illusion.

Those who know the mission of life and work like spiritual giants, for the liberation of all mankind, ever spreading the Light of God, who is all Love and Beauty, Truth and Goodness.

Those who walk the path of self-abnegation, with their hearts, minds and souls centred in God.

Those to whom the mundane world is a clogged toy, glittering but of no worth.

Those who conquer self to gain Self.

Those who transcend religion.

Those who are in communion with God and know God as the only Reality.

DISCOURSE NO. III

The Path of Asha

It is said whenever there is moral decadence among people, God sends His messengers on earth, to awake and teach them and bring them on the path of rectitude. Zoroaster who preached his religion in ancient Iran, about 9000 years ago, is considered historically, the first prophet on earth, who established a monotheistic religion. Other prophets followed at different intervals and in different countries, but the palm of glory naturally goes to Lord Zarthustra, who was the first in the rank of prophets to give divine truths to the world at large. This is an incontestable and irrefutable fact.

Lord Zoroaster is said to have led a life of austerity and seclusion for a number of years and he was able to commune with Lord Ahuramazda. This communion with God resulted in the establishment of Zoroastrianism, which is the most ancient religion in the world.

The first word spoken by Ahuramazda to Lord Zoroaster was Asha. Asha means righteousness, purity of mind, body and soul. This is the great mantra, which Zoroaster learnt from Ahuramazda, the King and Symbol of Righteousness.

"One alone is the Path — it is the Path of Righteousness." (Yesna 72-11)

Righteousness forms the bedrock of Zoroastrianism. The indispensability of this teaching of Righteousness was recognised by all other prophets that followed Zoroaster.

Ashem Vohu is one of the three *mahavakyas* in the holy scriptures of Zoroastrianism. Translated in English this short prayer means:

"Righteousness is good; it is best. Bliss exists (in the very heart of the universe). Bliss is for him who is righteous for the sake of righteousness."

To practise righteousness for the sake of righteousness and not from any ulterior motive, of gaining name or fame, wealth or riches, glory or power is the supreme teaching of Zoroaster. The sole idea of this great teaching is to take us to God — Ahuramazda, who is All Righteousness. We can not approach God, but through righteousness. If we love God and worship God, it can only be by practising righteousness in thought, word and deed. We can attune ourselves to God only through righteousness. It is a bond that binds us to God as well as to all good men on earth.

Got wants us His children to love Him and to worship Him without doubt, but he alone really has God in his heart who practises righteousness in thought, word and deed. The mantra of righteousness carried to its logical end is a mighty force, which binds us to everything in the universe from the star in the sky to the speck of dust on the ground. To attune ourselves to God and to all the holy ones and to all Nature is to liberate the forces of harmony and happiness which is the be-all and end-all of life and religion.

The word *"Yazmaida"* is frequently used in the daily prayer of a Zoroastrain. This is a most significant word. It means "May we be in tune with " i.e., to be in tune with God and all His creations, within and without, visible and invisible, including man's soul and man's spirit. But how could this harmony be effected? Only through purity of thought, word and deed — *Humakta, Hukhta, Huvarashta, Manasni, Gavasni, Kunasni.*

The following is a translation of the Nirang to the Khorshed and Meher Niyayish:

"All good thoughts, all good words, all good deeds are begotten of Budhi (the Highest Mind). All evil thoughts, all wicked words, all vicious deeds are not begotten to Budhi. Righteousness in thought, word and deed, leads to the Highest Existence. The be-all and end-all of pure thoughts, words and deeds is the Highest Existence. Such is the religion as known by the holy man."

Righteousness is of two kinds, internal and external. The external righteousness — Ashoi — Paki-e-tan deals with the question of outward cleanliness, which is also an essential factor in life. The *Vandidad,* is a highly instructive chronicle giving us minute details regarding observations of hygiene and sanitation in public and private life. The internal righteousness, which is called Ashoi-e-Ravan deals with the righteousness of the soul i.e. with moral and spiritual righteousness. Of-course, the latter takes precedence over the former and it is unwise, that emphasis should be laid on outside cleanliness of the body, to the neglect of the cleanliness of the soul. What matters most is not that you have polluted your fire, that you have not washed your hands and face, before partaking meals, that your women have not observed seclusion and rest during their menstruation period but whether your thoughts, words and deeds are righteous. What God wants is not only the cleanliness of the body but first and foremost the purity of heart. It is the heart that is the temple of God in the real sense of the word and not the fire-temple, where one may burn tons of sandalwood in the vain attempt to appease God.

It is through righteousness that man attains to divine knowledge. It is through righteousness that one can gain even the vision of God, the highest gift or boon which any man can attain to. It is supreme *Bliss*.

Righteousness is the seed of strength and power. A righteous man has God by his side and can do wonders. Righteousness is the sword by which the evil of unrighteousness can be slain and the world made happier and better for the progress of life.

The main teaching of Zoroastrianism is to raise a continuous crusade against evil. Evil is the demon, which has to be slain and destroyed by the propagation of truth and righteousness. In no religious scriptures is truthfulness and performance of promise held so sacred as in Zoroastrianism.

Righteousness is the pivot and pillar of Zoroastrianism.

"O Omniscient Lord! May I reach Thee by means of the holy mind. Grant me all the benefits of both the material and the invisible worlds which are obtainable through Righteousness, by means of which may be attained blissful happiness."

(Gatha Ahunavaiti 28-2)

The Gathas of Zarthustra, which are considered to be verses composed by Zoroaster himself are full of thoughts on Righteousness.

"Those who posses good wisdom, praise righteousness."

(Yasna Ha, 5-24)

When a Parsi ties the *kusti,* he puts two knots, one in front and one behind. The meaning of these knots is that the takes the vow to tie himself with other brothers and sisters of whatever nationality or country they be, and will speak truth and deal with all in a righteous manner.

Meekness, gentility and humility are offsprings of righteousness. Righteousness is the magnet that draws man to God.

"Through the best Asha, through the highest Asha, may we get a vision of Thee, may we draw near unto Thee, may we be in perfect union with Thee."

(Yasna 60-12)

Oh Ahuramazda, give us strength and wisdom to eschew evil and come to Thee triumphantly, following the path of Asha, the only Path to Thy Divine Abode.

DISCOUSE NO. IV

The Voice of Silence

Who would not like to hear the Voice of Silence, the soundless sound? The Voice of Silence is the Voice of God. Sitting alone on the banks of a river, underneath the canopy of the azure sky, studded with stars, and the bright moon, the queen among the stars, the gliding river makes a sweet murmuring music to the ear. The soft breeze that blows on the face and ruffles the hair, creates a happy lull in the mind, that turns wild thoughts to pastures new. The rumbling voice of the wind that sweeps through a distant forest and the moaning of the sea, that comes from afar make a medley of music too deep for words to describe.

It is only when the mind is silenced and the senses are curbed and the soul takes delight in Nature's joyous rides, that the Voice of the Self is heard. There is no music grander than the music of silent communion with the Inner Self.

The five senses and the mind screen the Self. Each one of us is a spark of God. Each one of us is a ray of the Universal Light. Each one of us is a drop of that Eternal Ocean which is God. For the drop to be merged into the Ocean, for the ray to be lost in the

Universal Light, for the spark to be absorbed in the Fire of God — this is the object and aim of life. To control the senses and the mind is the prerequisite, the *sine qua non* of the pilgrim's progress towards the Kingdom of Eternity.

To saunter in the pleasure ground of the senses is to instal the mind in the rough channels of life, leading to devastation and frustration. It is to incite the mind to slay the Self. Mind, not subjugated and controlled is the greatest barrier to Self-realisation.

God is Spirit. It is not with mundane eyes, that God can be seen and realised. It is the heart, the eye of the spirit, that alone can penetrate the veils and barriers and see God face to face.

It is heart, not the head, the inner illumination and not the reasoning faculty, which can cause the liberation of the soul. Ignorance is the mother of iniquity and misery. Knowledge is proud, that it knows so much, but in reality, it knows little.

We live in an age of Science, when war is still not banned and plays and important part in the economy of national life. In the ancient days, in Iran and India, kings were saints and sages. They knew the science of God — the true wisdom of the universe. They were adepts in mystical wisdom. This mystical wisdom, man in his pride today shuns, thinking that the modern civilization, — the growth of materialism — is a supreme test of his triumph, little knowing that the triumphs of mere material science, are ephemeral and what he worships is not true God, but false gods.

God is the Light that burns without a wick or fuel. It is the light that can never be blown by any gush of wind. To see this Light of Lights, requires a mind, disciplined by a life of self-abnegation and active altruism, cleaned and controlled by daily prayers, concentration and meditation. It is in the silence of mind, when the heart is enthralled and the soul is enflamed, that the secrets of the universe can be revealed — secrets which give the soul its sovereignty and unbounded powers for the good of all mankind.

Oh God, give us strength and courage to defy the wrong notions of life and lead a life of purity, prayers, active philanthropy and meditation, so that by curbing and slaying the mind, we may liberate our souls and the souls of our brothers and sisters. OM TAT SAT.

O God, we yearn to hear the music of Thy Voice, resounding and reverberating through the corridor of Eternity — the Voice of Divine Silence, that thrills and enthralls as we sit in deep communion with the stars and all the elements in the Cosmos, lost in deep reverie, in the mystic silence of the heart. It is like Silence speaking with Silence — the silence of the heart in deep communion with the Great Silence of the Universal Spirit.

DISCOURSE NO. V

Liberation from the Wheel of Birth and Death

When Buddha stirred out from the royal palace, leaving his young wife and child, bent upon finding a solution to many problems of life, he little knew, that he was destined by God to open before man's eyes, the way to salvation. He was full of milk of human kindness. Human misery and suffering so rampant in life made a deep impression upon his soul. He was convinced that life was no bed of roses but a bed-rock of throns and thistles. Disease, decay and death stalked the land, like grim ghosts, making a parody of life. What glittered was transient. Birth, decay and death seemed the inevitable way of the world. Was there a way out from the labyrinth of human suffering? Was there a way out from the wheel of birth and death ?

Buddha made penances and fasted for six long years to find a solution for himself for life's problem. He was reduced to a skeleton but all his austerities did not make him wiser in the least. He was still groping in darkness. He resolved however to change his tactics. He left off his penances and austerities and took to the golden, middling path. He make up his mind to give himself up to long meditation. He sat under the Bo tree determined not to leave the place till the object of his search had been found. He meditated for days sand nights and he was rewarded. He got illumination. He saw the doors of Nirvana open to him. He had the choice to leave the world of sin and sorrow, disease and death for good, but like a valiant soldier, he preferred to re-enter the arena of life and renew his struggles. He renounced his own freedom for the liberation of all mankind.

Buddha's great renunciation is one of the greatest in the history of saints, sages and prophets. He lived for more than forty years, after attaining ILLUMINATION and these golden years were spent in making a vigorous and prolific crusade against man's ignorance. There was nothing new in Buddha's teaching. The Law of Karma and Re-incarnation, upon which Buddha laid so much stress, were the very foundation stones of Hinduism. But in his time, Hinduism had lost its vigour, by the growth of false teachings and dogmas and foolish rites and rituals. Buddha discarded them and established his religion that was free from the mazes of metaphysics as well as from the foibles of rituals and ceremonies. His was a religion which preached purity of life and individual striving as the highest canon for reaching NIRVANA.

"Be a lamp unto thyself" preached the great Buddha. Be pure, be humble, restrain thy lower self, kill all desires, be fearless, be calm and placid like the ocean, that receives all rivers, that flow into it, without losing its sombre serenity. Such was the teaching of Buddha. The way to final freedom is within, said Buddha. Conquer self and thou shalt gain liberation, said Buddha. Buddha was concerned with the affairs of the soul and nothing beyond it. Deliverance of the soul from the bondage of physical birth was the theme of Buddha's teaching and he preached it by laying emphasis upon the delusive nature of the world and its attractions.

It is foolish to say that Buddhism is atheism. We shall not enter into any discussion on this great question but this much should be stated, that when Buddha got illumination, he knew more secrets of the universe than he cared to disclose or divulge to the world at large. An astute thinker, but at the same time a practical man, that he was, he took upon himself to preach that which appeared to him as the most salient factor viz., man's liberation from the wheel of birth and death. Buddha's code of ethics propounded to give effect to this teaching of the liberation of the soul is the soundest and the best in religious literature.

Buddhism is not atheism; it is neither pessimism — the two charges levelled against it. Buddha saw God face to face but he preferred not to disclose this secret, as his sole aim was to stimulate the mind of the people and get them away from tantacles of this world full of misery and suffering. His teaching aimed at the way to liberation from the dark clutches of *maya*.

This is our silent prayer to the great BRAHMAN, PURUSHOTTAMA, PARAMATMA, that He may give us strength, courage and resolute will to discard the *maya* of this world and strive with all our heart and soul, to attain to NIRVANA, by leading a life of purity, altruism, prayers, meditation and concentration.

Immortality

Who am I? Am I this body, this bundle of bones and flesh, nerves and arteries, tissues and cells, blood vessels and blood corpuscles? Am I the mind? Am I the senses? Why do I come to this world, wherefrom do I come and whither do I go? Is this world of *nama* and *rupa*, the real world? What is real: what is not real? What is eternal; what is not eternal? What is Vidya (wisdom); what is Avidya (ignorance)? Is it, that what we see with our naked eyes is the real or the unreal?

The Real is Invisible. It is the Absolute Spirit that pervades the universe. Deduct the whole from the whole and the remainder is still the whole. The Real is motionless, swifter than the mind. It is near; it far. It is within; it is without. It is bodiless. It is Omniscient. It is self-sprung. It is transcendental. It is immanent. It is eternal. It is infinite.

How to know this Spirit, which is Omnipotent, Omnipresent, Omniscient? This is the question of questions. But if you know Him, you know the secret of life, the secret of birth and death, the secret of attaining freedom from the bondage of this world, the secret of Immortality.

Brahman is the Absolute Spirit that transcends the universe. Atman is the Spirit that dwells in every human being. What is visible is not real. What is invisible is real.

This world is a delusion. It is a world of changing phenomena, impermanent and transient. The objects of the senses are of perishing nature. Each individual *jiva* is a spark of God. It makes its abode in the human body to gain experiences of the world. Its final destiny is union with God. It is immortal.

Divine knowledge, i.e. the Science of God is the highest wisdom. To know the Self is man's greatest achievement. How to gain this Divine Wisdom — this *Vidya* is the question.

The saints and sages of ancient Iran, the Rishis of India in the olden times, the philosophers of Greece who founded mystic schools, before the advent of Christ, and above all, those great prophets of yore who gave their religions to the world full of mystic thought and wisdom, were the pioneers in this occult science. The Upanishads, the Gita, Dhamapada, the Zand Avesta, the Bible (the old and new Testament), the Quran, — these are the mystic books, written in mystic languages, which describe the greatness of God and explain the real aim and object of life. To discard the Scriptures or to take them at their bare, face value, without delving deep into the innermost mysteries of their teachings is to lose the key to the inner realm of Divine Wisdom.

Occultism is the path of divine knowledge. What is latent is real, not what is patent. What is material is transient. It is spirit that is eternal, not matter.

The *Brahman gnan* can be attained only by those who discard self to gain the Self. A life of renunciation, purity of mind, humility, reverence, sincerity, courage, endurance, forgiveness, mercy, non-attachment, non-egotism, fearlessness, indifference and above all deep and abiding faith in the unity of God and non-separateness of life — these are the steps in the ladder of evolution that take one to the Supreme Abode of Immortality. He who loses life, gains life. He who gives away his all in all, gains eternity.

This whole world is covered by the Lord. Let us repeat this mantra, not once but a million times, till every part and parcel of our body, the mind, the heart and the soul, becomes vibrant with the thoughts of God. May we be absorbed, drowned and drenched in God, who is the only Reality — Eternal and Infinite. May we see God in everything. It is in this way our Atman shall be one with the Atman of all and gain immortality which is the sole aim and object of life.

DISCOURSE NO. VII

The Mystical "Seven"

Life's glamour is its mysticism. Mystical signs and emblems are the mystic language of the heart. They are the props of the mystic's life, the foundation of the mystic science.

The great Buddha meditated underneath the Bo tree and he got illumination. The Bo tree has therefore a special significance to the Buddhists and all those mystics who love God and who aspire for union with God through the path of prayers and meditation.

Seven is a great mystic figure which calls to memory sacred recollections. In Zoroastrian Scriptures, Ahuramazda is considered as the Head of the Seven Amshaspands. They are Ahuramazda, Bahman, Ardebahst, Sherewar, Asfandarmad, Khordad and Amardad. We shall not discuss the relative merits and powers of these great Celestial Beings, with Ahuramazda, as the Lord of Creation and Principal Amshaspand.

When the *Kundalini* serpent is awakened by meditation and concentration, it passes through seven *chakras*, one by one, till it reaches the last one situated in the crown of the head, which is called *Brahmanchakra* or the crown *chakra*. When it touches this salient point, the aspirant gets illumination. Their Sanscrit names are *Muladhara. Swathishtana, Manipura, Anahata, Vishuddha, Ajna* and *Sahasrara. Muladhara* is the basic or root *chakra* situated at the base of the spine. *Swathistana* is the Spleen *chakra,* situated, to be exact, a little below the naval. *Manipura* is the Naval *chakra* situated at the naval over the solar plexus. *Anahata* is the Heart *chakra,* situated over the heart. *Vishuddha* is the Throat *chakra,* situated at the front of the throat. *Ajna* is the Brow or Frontal *chakra* situated between the two eye-brows. And the last, *Sahasrara* is the Crown *chakra* on the top of the head. Thee *chakras* are connected with various *yogas,* the *Raja yoga,* the *Gnana yoga* and the *Bhakti yoga.* We need not go into details of this exceedingly interesting subject so well-known to those who aspire to walk with God.

According to medieval Christian theologists, there are seven deadly sins. They are Pride, Avarice, Wrath, Gluttony, Lust, Envy and Idleness. They are so very graphically described by Edmund Spencer in his immortal poem "Fairie Queene."

If there are seven deadly sins which according to medieval Christianity can be washed off by fast, prayers and almsgiving, there are seven virtues, which take man swiftly to the Path of Liberation. They are Faith, Hope, Love, Charity, Chastity, Truthfulness and Forgiveness. They are the petals of the lotus flower, shimmering on the waters of the ocean. The lotus is the holiest of the holy flowers — the greatest symbol of purity and spirituality.

The mystical "seven" reminds us of the Island of Seven Cities in the Atlantic. It is mentioned in some ancient history, that Christians persecuted by Saracens fled from their tyranny and took to sea. They were under the guidance of seven bishops and when they landed at some forlorn island in the Atlantic, they founded a colony and called it the Island of Seven Cities.

About the year 618 a hermit by name St. Kevin died in his cell in the Vale of Glendalough in Ireland and seven churches in most beautiful and ravishing architectural style, including monastic buildings were erected near his sepulchre. The remains of those magnificent edifices dedicated and consecrated to God are still extant.

What an electric thrill of joy passes through our body when we see a rainbow on the side of a mountain or in the sky. And this rainbow is made of seven colours.

Before the mariner's compass was discovered, the North Star was the only guide to the sailor on the stormy sea. In the cluster of stars, the North Star can easily be detected, by the situation of the Great Bear,— the contellation of Seven Stars.

How innocently does the girl plead "We are Seven" in that immortal poem of Wordsworth, the poet of Nature and the lover of God.

Seven indeed is a mystical and romantic number. Rome was built on seven hills and it was considered as eternal city. This tradition of its eternity was broken by the invasion of the Huns. Twice Attila, the

Hun came with his invading hordes to conquer Rome, but he withdrew, such was the effect of the tradition of Rome's Eternity. It was only at the third attempt, that the so called eternal city was subjugated by the sword of the infidel. It was not the infidel that had conquered Rome. It was because, the Romans taking to a life of pleasure and pride had deteriorated and declined in their morals to such an extent, that their downfall was inevitable.

Mystic charms have value only to those who aspire for mystical knowledge and mystical joy. It is our earnest prayer to Thee, Oh God, that Thy grace shall descend upon us and that our soul shall pass through the seven planes to reach Thy Abode of Eternity.

DISCOURSE NO. VIII

The Two Choices

The Bible says, "Draw nigh to God and He will draw nigh to you." (James IV-8) And it further says, "Friendship of the world is enmity with God. Whosoever therefore will be a friend of the world is the enemy of God." (James IV-4)

There are two factors ever working one against the other in the arena of life. They are the factors of Righteousness which leadeth to Light and Eternity and unrighteousness which leadeth to darkness and misery. Man has to make a choice between these two — whether he would like to listen to the voice of conscience, which is the Voice of God or follow the dictates of the senses and be caught in the snare of world's temptations. The two paths are distinctly opposite and they lead to different goals. To love God means to lead the life of spirit. To love the world and its allurements means to be a slave to the weaknesses of the flesh. The former opens the way to the liberation of the soul. The latter drags the soul down and ties it to the wheel of birth and death. If one seeks God, who is LOVE, LIGHT and GLORY, he rises step by step in the ladder of evolution and reaches Eternity. If he seeks the applause of the world, its tinsels and allurements, he falls and is lost in the abyss of darkness. He who sees God in every living being and is meek, kind and loving, pure in heart, noble in soul, fearless, unselfish and self-sacrificing, reaches the highest rung of the ladder in the evolution of life. The one who prefers world's giddy pleasures, eats cakes of husks, not flour and dies in sin and sorrow, to return again to this alluring world to make atonement for his sins of omission and commission.

God, not mammon, Light not darkness. Joy not misery — is the goal of life. The prophets have spoken in the name of the Lord and given to us golden teachings for our edification and enlightenment. He is really deaf and blind, who hears not the Voice of God that is within him and who sees not God, in all that is Holy and Beautiful and Glorious in life.

God should be our "consuming fire." He is our helper. Let us seek His grace with reverence and "Godly fear."

"God loveth. He chasteneth and scourgeth every son whom He receiveth." (Hebrews 12,6.) Better to bear the scourges of God and be chastened for final victory than be deluded by the *maya* of the world and be lost in the abyss of darkness and gloom, misery and degradation.

To submit to God's will is the way to ultimate victory and triumph of the soul. Jerusalem! What does this word signify? Islam! What does this word mean? Jerusalem means submission to the will of God. Islam also means the same thing. In fact, submission to the will of the Lord is the keynote of the teaching of all main religions, whether Zoroastrianism or Hinduism, Christianity or Islam.

Christ gave two commandments;

(1) "Thou shalt love the Lord, thy God with all thy heart, and with all thy soul and with all thy mind.

(2) Thou shalt love thy neighbour as thyself."

If only these two commandments were followed, it would open to the human soul the doors of inward knowledge beyond human understanding and comprehension.

Blessed are the meek, blessed are the poor in spirit, blessed are those who hunger for righteousness, blessed are they who are pure in heart, blessed are they who are peace makers, blessed are they who even when they are persecuted, reviled, scoffed at and scorned for their righteousness and love of God, desist not from the path of rectitude even a little. They are the salt of the earth. They are the light of the world.

Oh God, give us wisdom to eschew evil and to work for the triumph of the spirit against all odds in life. We shall follow Truth and nothing but Truth, for Truth alone can make us free.

"By means of the highest and noblest righteousness, O Ahuramazda, may we have Thy vision, Thy proximity, Thy eternal friendship." (Yasna Ha, 60.11, 12.)

DISCOURSE NO. IX

Birth and Death

The two most important and mystical events in a man's life are birth and death. It is a mystery how man enters in this physical life and it is a mystery where he goes to, when he leaves the physical plane. This mystery of birth and death is revealed to one who understands the Science of God.

Man is spirit, not matter. The whole universe is an emanation from One Supreme Absolute SPIRIT or IDEA. This Absolute Spirit pervades the whole universe. If we fix our attention on this one point of supreme importance that there is One BEING in the whole Cosmos, we realise the Truth of Truths. This ONE becomes Many and we see the play of multiple forces giving rise to multiple forms of diverse nature.

Man is spirit. He is an emanation from God — the Absolute Spirit. He is a spark of God. This spark in its journey from the Spiritual Plane, takes sheaths, as it descends through the various intervening planes, as it is extremely difficult for pure spirit to live as such, unless it is clothed by the matter of which the planes are composed viz. Budhic, Mental and Astral.

When the soul, the *jiva* takes birth in the human body, it is essentially clothed and wrapped up in various sheaths, the physical, etheric, astral, mental and budhic. The Hindu Scriptures speak of these sheaths — the various *Koshas*. The Theosophists also agree that the *Monad*, the spark of God, is covered in sheaths as above when it enters into the physical body.

The sole aim and object of life is that the soul entrenched in its sheaths, must come out from these sheaths. It must lose the sheaths one by one. Each sheath is a bondage to the plane to which it belongs.

When death takes place and the silvery cord which binds the astral with the physical body, is severed, the soul leaves the physical body and it drops the various bodies as it ascends from one plane to another except the *Anandamaya Kosha*, the sheath of *Maya* (delusion), which it retains, for it has to come back again to this physical world unless it has already attained its liberation.

The birth and death is a presentation of the picture of sheaths formed from the matter of various planes. The soul takes these sheaths when it takes birth in human body. When it leaves the body, it discards these sheaths, one by one. After physical death, it enters the astral plane in the astral sheath. When it discards the astral sheath, it means astral death and it goes to the higher plane in the mental sheath and so on.

This physical plane is the School of Experiences for the soul. This is the most important plane, for, the liberation of the soul from the chain of birth and death, can be achieved on this plane and none other. One should therefore recognise the extreme importance of physical life on this earth plane. It has not to be squandered in empty tinsels but in achieving liberation which is the goal of life.

Heaven and Hell are mere allegorical terms. There are no such things as eternal flames of hell that are created by God to consume sinful souls. There is no such thing as Heaven made of diamond houses, with rivers of milk and honey flowing perennially. The evil we do, we leave behind. But we carry with us the seeds of noble thoughts and noble actions, our self-denial and sacrifice. These noble thoughts of self-abnegation take us to happier planes and the soul enjoys the fruit of good actions on the earth plane on the other planes, as it advances, according to its capacity, from the astral, to the mental, the higher mental and the spiritual.

The marriage of the soul and the spirit takes place when the soul is perfected and it gains *nirvana* and it no longer comes back on its pilgrimage to the earth plane. But if the liberation is not achieved, the soul once again takes the round and comes to the physical plane. It goes through various experiences of life, according to its past *karma*.

This world is a world of suffering. And Buddha gave the *mantra* of how to avoid this continuous suffering by seeking liberation from the wheel of birth and death.

Oh God, give us courage and strength to do our duties in this life, to submit ourselves every minute, to Thy Will, fixing our gaze on THEE and THEE alone, so that purifying our heart, mind and soul, we may reach soon the goal of NIRVANA, the goal of MOKSHA, in this very round of life.

DISCOURSE NO. X

The Four Paths

Nachiketas seeks no boon save knowledge of the Hereafter. Yama promises long life with all the enjoyments of the world but the lad refuses them. His mind is bent upon immortality. All that is ephemeral and transient, he discards as of no worth. He says: "Oh Death, tell us that for which men have doubt, and which is about the Great HEREAFTER. Nachiketas does not choose any other boon but that (concerning the soul) of which the knowledge is hidden." (Kathopanishad Chapter 1–29).

It is only the wise who seek that which is real. God alone is Real. When Jesus had fasted for full forty days and forty nights and was feeling very hungry, he was tempted by the devil. He said: "If thou be the Son of God, command that these stones be made bread." But calm and untempted, Jesus replied to him: "It is written, Man shall not live by bread alone, but by every word that proceedeth out of the mouth of God."

The aspirant who seeks the Kingdom of Heaven — the vision of God, — God-realisation, should not be daunted by the difficulties of the path. Is it not said in the Bible; "And I say unto you, Ask, and it shall be given you; seek, and ye shall find; knock, and it shall be opened unto you." (St. Luke XI–9) All that is wanted is the earnest and burning desire in the aspirant to realise God.

To know Brahman is to become one with Brahman. In the Hindu Scriptures, there are four paths described, which lead to salvation. They are: (1) *Karma Yoga*, (2) *Bhakti Yoga*, (3) *Gnana Yoga* and (4) *Raja Yoga*. The object of all these *yogas* is to make the aspirant realise that all indeed is BRAHMAN.

"With the mind harmonised by yoga, he sees the Self abiding in all beings and all beings in the Self, he sees the same everywhere." (Bhagvad Gita, Discourse VI-29)

"He who being established in unity, worships Me, who dwells in all beings, that yogis abides in Me, whatever his mode of living may be." (Bhagvad Gita, Discourse VI–31)

The popular idea is that to realise God one should renounce everything, that he must leave *Samsara* and go to the forest and live by himself in utter solitude and renunciation. The Gita says, this is not necessary. The aspirant can realise God, whatever his mode of living may be. Renunciation does not mean cutting oneself off from the world. He should live in the world but he should not be of the world. True renunciation is detachment of the mind.

A *Karma Yogi* is one who lives in the wor ld, works whole-heartedly for the betterment of the world, with his mind fixed on God, all the time. He works but without any kind of attachment and without expectation of any fruit thereof. He works for the sake of work. He does his duties, whether they be performance of religious ceremonies, social duties, home duties, or political duties. His sole concern is to work for the sake of God and for the amelioration of the lot of suffering humanity without any kind of gain for himself. He is not concerned, if he succeeds or fails. He does not care, if he is applauded or censured. He is absolutely indifferent to praise or dispraise. He may be a King like Janaka or a fakir in rags. He may be living in a palace or a hut. Whatever may be his mode of life — whether he be born with a golden spoon in his mouth or a leaden spoon, whether he puts on a silken dress or a saffron robe, it is immaterial, so long as he can control his mind and has absolutely a detached outlook and is impervious to his own interest. Self-interest is completely obliterated in a *karma yogi*.

This kind of yoga soon purities the mind, the heart and the soul and qualifies the aspirant for God-realisation. All religions place very great importance upon this yoga of Action. Zoroaster, Krishna, Buddha, Christ and Mohammed may be considered as the greatest and best exponents of this yoga, though it must be said, they were masters of divine wisdom and knew that there were other paths open which could lead the aspirant to the Temple of Divinity.

The second *margha* of which the Gita speaks in such eloquent terms is *Bhakti Yoga*. Just as *Karma Yoga* appeals to a man of action, *Bhakti Yoga* appeals to a man of emotion. In each one of us, there is a certain tendency, which predominates over other traits in our character and it is necessary that the aspirant must follow that path for which he is suited temperamentally.

Bhakti Yoga, to all intents and purposes is the easiest and safest path. The *Bhaktas* have no desire for life or death. They have no selfish interests of any kind. Their devotion to God is so deeply rooted that the whole world appears to them as non-existent. They become so God-intoxicated, that they live for God and God alone. God alone is their vocabulary, their only thought, their only desire, their only target. They offer themselves whole heartedly to God. They worship Him. They pray to Him day and night. They build a golden temple in their heart and are absorbed in saying *mantras* and *japas* and in prayers and meditation. The Gita says: "Fix thy mind on Me, be devoted to Me, bow down to Me, having thus united thy (whole) Self to Me, taking Me as the Supreme Goal, thou shalt come to Me." (Discourse IX-34.)

The third path or the *margha* is called *Gnana Yoga.* This is meant for one, who is a philosopher, who wants to realise God by philosophical reasoning. This is a difficult path but to a yogi, who is bent upon acquiring the knowledge of the Brahman, nothing is so difficult. Shankaracharya and Ramanuja, who have made such solid contribution to the Scriptural literature of the Hindus, may be considered as the greatest exponents and propagandists of *Gnana Yoga.* The whole of the Vedanta Philosophy is a product of Indian Rishis who have made tremendous contribution to world's spiritual literature. Aldous Huxley rightly considers the Vedanta Philosophy as Perennial Philosophy and he has solid grounds for making such a universal statement. It is a philosophy of philosophies which no distance of time would ever impair or eclipse. This ancient Indian philosophy should be the basis of the Universal Religion, which must in the course of time take birth, by unifying all religions and all mankind under one fold.

The fourth Path is that of *Raja Yoga*. This *yoga* is the king of all yogas. The chief point in this yoga is the preponderant attention paid to meditation. And to be frank, whether a man may be a *Karma Yogi*, a *Bhakti Yogi* or a Gnana Yogi, meditation to obtain the goal of Self-realisation is indispensable. Meditation is the key that opens the gates to the secret knowledge of the soul and the universe.

Unfortunately grave abuse is made, when people meditate for the simple purpose of gaining *siddhies* i.e. miralculous powers of flying in the air or walking on the waters and so forth. The object of meditation is union with God and not to obtain miraculous powers and to make an exhibition of them or parade them out of vaingloriousness. A true *Raja Yogi* is the highest yogi for he makes use of his transcendental powers in secrecy, for the benefit of all mankind.

Oh God, this is our earnest prayer to Thee, that Thou in Thy great mercy, shalt show us the way, by which we may come to Thee and be united with Thee for ever, whether it be by the *Karma margha*, *Bhakti margha*, *Gnana margha* or *Raja yoga* or by the combination of any or all of them.

DISCOURSE NO. XI

The Way to Salvation by Disinterested Action

Karma Margha

This is world of sin and sorrow, distress and misery. Let us wipe the tear of the orphan. Let us feed the hungry and clothe the naked. Let us console the sorrowing widow with words of wisdom and of love. Let us stay the hand of the sinner and put him on the path of righteousness. Let us turn away wrath with a gentle word and smile. Let us scatter the clouds of slander and bring peace and harmony. Let us cheer the weary and the wayward, the sick in body and in soul. Let us guide the footsteps of the unweary and stop the squanderer from his evil ways. Let us help the deaf and the blind, the lame and the leper. Let us assuage the pain and suffering of the ailing. Let us sing the song of joy and beatitude and utter the name of God, the talisman for all ills of life. Let us bring a ray of radiance in all the dark slums and alleys of life. We shall not then have lived in vain.

Let us be content to lead a lonely life in the midst of storm and tussle, unmindful of world's praise or dispraise. The silent moon in the silvery night and the radiant sun in the day are the witnesses of our silent deeds of love and mercy. They are the plenipotentiaries of God, seeking to bring light in the dark alleys of life.

Souls hungry for spiritual food and thirsting for spiritual water need our succour. Let us help the sickly souls in the hour of their distress and lift them to God, the Supreme Deity. Let us tie the wounds of the wounded and the ailing. Let us befriend the friendless and father the orphan and the naked. Let us put on the armour of Truth and dispel the forces of darkness, by radiating love and light in the cells and slums of human suffering. Let us build temples of love in the hearts of our brethren. Let us be the Torchbearers in the struggle of life and fight for God, Ahuramazda, against the dark forces of Satan and Ahreman. Let us be the Standardbearers of Joy. Let us illumine the hearts and minds and souls of men and women with God's love and light. This is the way to Salvation. This is *Karma Yoga*.

O God, give us courage and wisdom to fight the battle of life and save ourselves from the whirlpool of word's delusion. It is only when we grow in spirit, we realise what is real and permanent and what is unreal and impermanent. O God, give us the inner sight, for that is the lamp we need to escape from *maya's* den and find a way to Thy Abode of Eternity.

DISCOURSE NO. XII

The Path of Devotion

Bhakti Margha

Love is the acid test of human life. It is a seed of sacrifice. It is a harmonising unit. It is a great factor in the progress of life. It sublimates the mind, makes a man, a hero, a dauntless champion of the weak against the strong. When man loves man and is a brother to him, not in mere name but in reality, he becomes a God.

Love is divine. The Bible says, "Love thy neighbour as thyself," but above all, love God, the Creator of the Universe, the Father of all humanity. To love God, to offer our whole-hearted devotion to Him, to concentrate our mind on Him, to consecrate and dedicate our heart and soul to God who is Universal and Absolute, Personal and Impersonal, Manifest and Unmanifest, Transcendent and Immanent, is to stimulate all the inner forces in us, which seek outlet for expression.

People worship God in various ways. To some, religious rites and ceremonies appeal the most and they burn incense and sanalwood in the temples and the churches, where they congregate to offer prayers to God, the Almighty, in the spirit of devotion and humility. They build temples to God and give their best to these temples. They are the embodiment and centre of their heart's devotion. The church architecture, the church music, the church paintings, the church artistry, manifest the sublimity of man's soul, eager to express and give its best for the adornment and beauty of the House of God.

There are others who feel that it is better to raise the temple in one's own heart, for the Great Spirit dwells in him. He is a lover of Nature. He is a lover of all that is beautiful and serene, musical and calm. He seeks God not in man-made temples and mosques but in the wide vistas of Nature, in the solitude of his heart, underneath the canopy of the serene sky, in Nature's corners of exquisite beauty. He prays alone, by the side of a running brook or near the seashore. His inward voice of devotion mingles with the voice of Nature — the moaning sea and the murmuring brook. His soul is in tune with Nature. He is devoured by the all consuming fire of divine emotion. His whole heart is absorbed in God. His mind is drenched in thoughts of God. His soul is bathed in the halo of God's resplendent Light and Glory. To him the world is a holy tavern where he can drink the cup of immortal wine and commune with his Beloved in ecstatic delight. God is the centre and target of his heart. Pure in mind, he has no love for the tinsels of life. Having conquered all desires of the flesh, his only aim and object is to worship God in the temple of his heart. He is God-intoxicated; God mad. He shuns society and life's giddy ways. He is a seeker after Truth, but through the path of devotion only. God, God and God alone is his thought. God is his food; God is his drink; God is his raiment. He wants nothing but God.

The *bhakta* sees God everywhere, — in the sun and the sky, the moon and the stars, the river that swiftly flows and falls into the ocean and the mountain that stands in its majestic sublimity, soaring high to the sky, pointing the way to man to rise higher and higher in life. He sees God in the flower that blooms, in the stag that runs about and the child that smiles. He sees God in all that is serence, calm and beautiful. He tunes his soul with Nature's rhythmic music, to stimulate his inner spirit to worship God who is the Lord of his heart and the Lord of the universe.

Fakir or king, the true devotee to God must ultimately feel the call within him and give up everything of the world, — his all in all, to serve God, to worship God, with all his heart and mind and soul, without the least thought of to-morrow and in utter self-abnegation. The wide sky is his canopy. The earth is his bed. The sea that makes a mourning sound and the trees in the forest that make a rustling music as the wind sweeps through the jungle, are his companions. God in his Friend, in this friendless world of ours. God is his Guide in this tractless desert of our life. His love for God, his devotion to God are his greatest treasures. He lives in God; he lives for God; he works for all humanity in the silence of his heart for the sake of God. God is the Be-All and End-All of life.

"I am the Self, O Gudakesha, seated in the hearts of all beings. I am the beginning, the middle and also the end of all beings." (Bhagvad Gita-Discourse X–20)

Om Tat Sat

Oh God, give us strength and wisdom to consecrate and dedicate our heart solely to Thee. Thou art the consuming fire. Thou art the Sun of our worship. May we worship Thee whole-heartedly and devotedly and come to Thee by the Margha of *Bhakti*.

DISCOURSE NO. XIII

The Path of Wisdom
Gnana Margha

Rationalists pin their faith on their reasoning capacity and anything that is beyond reason is discarded by them. Can God be realised by mere intellect? Scientists have tried this method and have failed undisguisedly. But we have evidence of the existence of God. His Omnipotence, Omnipresence, Omniscience through seers and sages who have realised Self.

The teachings of a God-realised man are therefore of extreme importance. They are of uniform nature. For vital truths, revealed by God to man can not but be of the same uniform nature. The *Upanishads* and the *Bhagvad Gita* are monumental books, giving God's truths, as revealed by Him to Indian *Rishis* of old. India's spiritual wealth lies in the galaxy of God-realised persons, that this ancient country, true to its traditions has produced. We bow down to these *Rishis*, the dead and the living, our preceptors and gurus, who have shown us the path of salvation.

Greater than the senses is the mind. Greater than the mind is buddhi, intuition. Greater than buddhi is the *Atman*. The Atman is the spark of God, that dwells within man. Greater than the Atman is *Avyaktam,* the unmanifested God. And beyond this Avyaktam is Purusha, Brahman, the Absolute Spirit, that pervades the universe. He who knows Him attains salvation and immortality.

God is one but He manifests Himself in diverse ways. The essence of everything in the universe, if we subtract its name and form, — *nama* and *rupa,* — is God. The God without is called Brahman. The God within is called Atman. He is both transcendent and immanent.

A man is not what he is personally known by his name. John, Sitaram or Feredun, — these are mere outward names, given to personalities for the purpose of earthly distinction only. Man is not the der. The real in him is the Atman within him. But for the Atman, the body, the senses and the mind would not function. They have no separate existence. When we see a person, we must realise that he is not what he is known by his name, but Atman. If we gain this knowledge that everything is Atman, we come to this inescapable conclusion, that all is God. Nonseparateness of life and unity of God are the singular teaching of Spiritual Philosophy. God is One. Life is One. There is no separateness between man and man, between man and God. Non-separateness is the key to salvation. To know God is to become liberated and gain immortality.

How can God be known? He is the ear of ears; He is the eye of eyes. But we can never see Him with our physical eyes or hear Him with our physical ears.

Our senses and our mind are useless weapons in cognising God. Nay, they are impediments in gaining the knowledge of God. The five senses and the mind are to be subjugated. The desires have to be overcome completely.

"The Self can not be reached by speech, by mind, or by ear." (Kathopanished Valli VI—12). No amount of logical argumentation or reasoning will bring the aspirant, near to the goal, even by an iota. It is only by implicit faith in God and by the guidance of those sages and saints who have realised God, that divine knowledge can be attained. Practice of celibacy, austerity, detachment and desirelessness are very necessary. The knots of false knowledge have to be untied. Selfishness has to give way to unselfishness, pride for humility, love for pleasures for a life of seclusion and austerity. Love for power, self and glory has to be completely annihilated and instead, the virtues of sacrifice, non-egotism, charity, and purity of mind, body and soul are to be practised. "When all desires that dwell in the heart, cease, the mortal becomes immortal and atman, Brahman."

(Kathopanishad—Valli VI—14.)

One of the greatest obstacles in the attainment of immortality is man's egotism. This has to be crushed and pounded to dust. No man should take pride in any achievement. He is not the doer. It is God, who makes him an instrument for the progress of His Plan.

We know the beautiful story related in Kenopanishad. The Devas won a great victory over the Asuras. They thought is was their victory. They said: "To us, belongs the victory, to us belongs the glory." Brahman to teach them a lesson appeared to them in the form of a Great Spirit. They did not know that it was *Brahman*.

Agni, the God of Fire, approached the Great Spirit and said haughtily: "I am *Agni*. I can burn to ashes whatever is on earth." Brahman held out before him a blade of grass and asked him to burn it. But how-soever much he tried, he could not burn it. Crest-fallen and dejected, he went back to his companions and told them the story of his impotence. *Vayu*, the God of Wind volunteered them to approach the Spirit. The latter held out a blade of grass and asked *Vayu* to blow it off. The God of Wind tried his best, but all his power was in vain. He too was humiliated and he returned to his colleagues and told the story of his failure.

Indra the head of the Devas, then stirred out with the determination to find out who the Spirit was. But the great Spirit, did not even care to talk to him. It disappeared. Indra was utterly humiliated and felt the pang of remorse, the most. He was bewildered and lost in a maze of confusion. It was then he got the knowledge, that the Great Spirit was Brahman and that because of Brahman, he and his comrades won the victory over the *Asuras*. It was not their victory, for which they should take glory but God's victory.

Knowledge of Self is necessary for the attainment of *Moksha*. He attains that knowledge who discards what is transient and perishable and clings to that which is eternal and imperishable. He who meditates upon Brahman, in purity of heart, mind and soul, taking the word *OM*, as indicating Brahman — and this word is a most appropriate sound symbol of Brahman — he attains the goal of immortality. It is only by incessant meditation, that God can be revealed to man.

Oh God, it is our most fervent prayer, that Thou shalt give us strengh to realise Thee, manifest or unmanifest. We shall not slacken our efforts, even by an iota and shall reach Thee by the *Margha of Gnana.*

DISCOURSE NO. XIV

The Path of Meditation

Raja Yoga

We have already dealt with three paths that lead to salvation. They are all spoken of in the Gita viz. the *Karma Yoga*, the *Bhakti Yoga* and *Gnana Yoga*. But the fourth and the most important path is *Raja Yoga*, the King of all *Yogas*.

Says the Gita: "Howsoever men approach Me, even so do I reward them. My path do men follow in all things, O son of Pritha."

(Discourse IV—II).

God wants every one to come to Him, by selecting any path he likes. The various religions founded in the world are the paths, by which the respective votaries of those religions, in which they are born should strive to reach the goal. For what is the object of religion? It is to stir the soul to its very depth and make is conscious of its immortality. The principal factor are Will i.e. volition, Feeling i.e. emotion and Understanding i.e. intellection. All these three parts in man are to be developed to the highest extent. There should be a harmonious development of man, as a whole, though it must be admitted at the same time, that that characteristic which plays the most dominant part in individual temperament should be given first preference and fully developed. These characteristics or traits differ in different individuals. It is therefore that we have different paths, though really speaking a harmonious and simultaneous development of all characteristics viz man's Will, Feeling and understanding, is necessary.

It is the function of religion to educate man's soul in its entirety. Man is not only feeling, understanding or will but a combination of them all and as such the purpose of religion, philosophy, or the higher science of divine Truth, by whatever name you call it, is to educate the soul as a whole and not deal with its parts separately.

Raja Yoga is a most wonderful *yoga*. It is the highest of all the *yogas*, for it aims at development of man's soul in its entirety. This *yoga* is open to all, whether he is a *Karma yogi*, a *bhakta*, or a *gnani*. It is considered to be partly a psychological and partly a physiological method of worship. Its fundamental purpose is to regulate the breath and control the mind. The Indian *Rishis* divide *Raja Yoga* into eight parts. Patanjali calls it the *yoga* of either limbs. They are:

(1) *Yama*, which consists in the practice of the following virtues viz. non-violence, truthfulness, chastity, non-receiving of gifts and non-stealing.

(2) *Niyaman*, which insists upon the observance of cleanliness, contentment, austerities, study of sacred Scriptures and self-surrender to God.

(3) *Asana*, postures, such as are convenient for practice of concentration.

(4) *Pranayama*, control of breath.

(5) *Pratyahara*, that which makes the mind introspective.

(6) *Dharana*, concentration of mind.

(7) *Dhyana*, meditation.

(8) *Samadhi*, deep meditation roecstatic state of supersensuous consciousness

The goal of *Raja Yoga* is *Samadhi*. We shall not discuss here the method of awakening the *Kundalini*, the Serpent Fire or the *Chakras*. All we wish to say is, that as far as possible, artificial methods of forcing internal development, by regulating breath should be avoided. The more determined, and a spirant is to quicken his progress on the path, the better it is for him. But he should avoid artificial methods, as they are most dangerous and under no circumstances, should be practised without the guidance of a Self-realised man. A *guru*, a Master, whether in physical body or in spirit form is absolutely necessary. It is only the guru, that can put the *chela* on the path and when once the latter enters into the stream, the *guru* remains his preceptor and guide till the last.

There are various Initiations on the Path. Each initiation marks a certain progress of the soul. Generally, it takes seven incarnations, for the soul, once it is established on the Path, under the guidance of a *guru,* to reach the goal. But it all depends upon the efforts of the aspirant himself. He may take seventy incarnations instead of seven, if he is lethargic. But if he is vigilant, forceful and determined to cut short his journey, he can reach the goal even in one incarnation.

Meditation is the key to the Invisible Realms of God. It leads to expansion of consciousness. It bestows upon the aspirant psychic and miraculous powers. He can cross the sea. He can fly in the air. He can hear people speaking in distant lands. He can read a man's thoughts and see his *aura*. He can foretell. He can heal the sick and the ailing. He can be buried underneath the ground for several hours and still not die.

The objective of *Raja Yoga* is not attainment of miraculous powers. He who meditates for personal aggrandisement, to satisfy his personal vanity and to achieve personal liberation is not a true *yogi*. He is the truest of the true *yogis*, who meditates day and night, renouncing everything for the higher purpose of attaining union with God and those powers, which are necessary, to enable him to work for the liberation of others. He seeks liberation not from the selfish object of satisfying his own inner craving, but to liberate humanity, by perfecting this imperfect world of ours, by bringing the light of God in the dark cells and alleys of life.

Let us bow down to these great souls, — the *Jivanmuktas* — the Gurus of humanity, who having renounced their own immortality, work in this plane of ours, silently and unostentatiously, under the direct guidance of God, with whom they are united, for the good of all humanity. When a man reaches this state of *Jianmukti* — the highest is the evolution of human life, nothing is hidden from him. He enters into fullness of life. There is no barrier, no veil between him and the hidden worlds. He becomes omnipotent and omniscient, so far as this world is concerned. His is the life of spirit. He cares not for forms. Distinction has no place in his vision or in his vocabulary. All are one, for there is no separateness in life. He is the Master of Compassion. He stays in this plane of sin and suffering of his own accord, to raise men from the mud of *maya* to the great Light of God — Immortality.

Oh God, this is our fervent prayer, that we may evolve ourselves, by following the path of renunciation and meditation to reach the goal of liberation and after becoming *Jivanmuktas* we may serve manking for their liberation.

DISCOURSE NO. XV

God and *Maya* (Nature)

God is eternal. He is *Sat Chit Ananda* — Absolute Existence, Consciousness, Bliss. He who rules out God from the programme of his life, is to be pitied. He is miserable. He is ignorant. He purses shadows, not substance. He is a victim to illusion. He is a slave to shallow reasoning. Reasoning is like candle light. The higher intellect — *buddhi,* intuition is sun light. Intuition is the third eye, the eye of the mystic, the divine eye, the secret talisman, that opens the doors to the hidden wealth of the universe.

Man in his ignorance and vanity may take pride, that he is the doer. But it is not so, Man is not, what appears to be, a composition and bundle of mind and body, senses and nerves, tissues and blood-vessels. They are of perishing nature. The eternal in man is the *Atman,* the Spirit, the *Farohar,* which dwells in the human soul and is a silent witness to all the actions of the soul. The *Atman* is Spirit, unborn, eternal. It can not be created or manufactured like a pot from clay or woven like a piece of cloth from cotton yarn. He is causeless.

It is the *Atman* in man that enables the various organs of the human body and the mind to function.

But for It, they would perish and die. All is therefore *Atman*. To know the *Atman* is to gain the elixir of life.

"The *Atman* subtler than the subtle, greater than the great, is seated in the heart of every living being. He who is free from desire, with the mind and the senses composed, beholds the Majesty of the Self and becomes free from sorrow."

(Kathopanishad, Valli II—20).

The *Atman* is the Lord of the Chariot. The body is the chariot. Intellect, *Buddhi* is the charioteer. Mind is the rains. The senses are horses and their objects are the roads. If the horses are controlled properly, the charioteer enjoys a happy ride. But if the senses are not controlled by the mind, the chariot is dashed to pieces and life becomes a heap of ruins. It is a struggle between *Vidya* and *Avidya*. *Vidya* is knowledge of the Self, discrimination. Avidya is ignorance, want of control.

The greatest demon on earth plane is *Avidya*. There is no monster that stalks the land so unabashed and causes cataclysms of misery and horror as Ignorance. By ignorance, we mean ignorance of the knowledge of God. A rustic, with love for God and all that is holy pure and simple is more learned than the septic, who boasts of his scientific knowledge and discoveries but withholds his homage to God, the Great creator, who is the cause of the manifestation of the whole universe. Knowledge without the understanding of God. His Omnipotence, Omnipresence, Omniscience, His Beauty. His Grace, His Love, His Compassion, is trash. It is mere husk, not flour. It is shadow, not substance.

It is darkness, not light. It is misery, not happiness. It is mud, not gold.

The Gita says: "Though I am unborn of imperishable nature and though I am the Lord of all beings, yet ruling over My own Nature, I am born by My own *Maya*." (Discourse IV—6). Man being bound down to the Law of *Karma*, has to take birth. He is swayed by the three *gunas* and Nature, *Prakriti* holds him in its grasp. In the case of God, it is not so. He has *Maya* under perfect control. He rules Maya, *Prakriti*, Nature. Even when it appears, that He has taken birth and is embodied through His own *Maya*, it should be realised that in reality it is not so. His embodiment in *Maya* is only an outward phenomenon of passing nature.

His divine nature can not be affected in the least. He is the Lord and Controller of *Maya* and *Prakriti*.

When there is a rise of unrighteousness and decay of morals, God manifests Himself. We know of Lord Krishna, how He came on earth on his divine mission to dispel darkness and misery and bring in light and happiness. We know of Christ's mission on earth. He came to teach man, to love God and his neighbour and to establish the Kingdom of Righteousness. He was the saviour of the world, "a good shepherd, who gave his life for the sheep." He said: "As the Father knoweth me, even so know I the Father." "I and My Father are one" was his announcement to the people and his mission was to make all men One with God. "Father is in me and I in Him," so often Christ said and he gave his life. He was crucified, for people could not understand his great mission and his greatness.

The Gita says: "Whenever there is decay of righteousness, O Bharata and rise of unrighteousness, then I manifest Myself.

For the protection of the good, for the destruction of the wicked and for the establishment of righteousness, I am born in every age."

(Discourse IV—7 and 8).

This world is a delusion and unless we slay this delusion with the knowledge of God, we can never attain immortality, which is the goal of life.

When the silvery moon shines in the blue vault of the sky and the stars cast their starry light, when nature is hushed into serence quietness and there is stillness all around, the soul is stirred and our thoughts and aspirations go to the Great Brahman, whose Spirit pervades the whole universe. We hear the still, small voice, that comes from the cavity of the heart. It is the voice of Atman. It is the inner voice, which we can hear only, if we have succeeded in subjugating our mind and the senses, which are the greatest mischief makers in this world of ours. Slay the senses and the mind — this is the slogan, which one must follow, if he wishes to escape from the *maya* of this world, the cause of all sin and sorrow, misery and distraction.

This is our fervent prayer to God to give us insight into the inner knowledge of the Self, so that knowing Self, we may be liberated from the thraldom of this world of *maya*.

God's Light

I stay on this earth plane,
Unaffected by pleasure or pain.
With God as my Friend and Ally,
My soul is free, anywhere to fly.

Unfetterd, serene and calm,
I see good in all, without harm.
God's serene voice I hear
Without any fear or tear.

The silvery moon and the shinning stars,
The Jupiter, the Great Bear and the Mars.
And all the Constellations and the flaming Fire,
Stir my soul to fly higher and higher.

In the silence of the silvery night
I pray to God with all my might.
He is the pilot of my ship,
As I sail on the waters of the deep.

He is Love; He is Light;
He is the jewel of my heart.
Unborn, eternal, causeless,
He is the soul of goodness, faultless.

Spirit and Matter

Man seeks individuality. He wants to put the stamp of personality on himself. He is guided or rather misguided by the serene voice of *maya* and he feels that he has a right of individual existence. He strives for his own gain. He works for his own glory. He lives in a world, where he hears the echo of "My and mine." This is my house, my city, my country. I did this. I did that. I wrote this fine play. I won the match. I built this church. I founded this hospital. I raised funds for the school. I won the prize. I am the chairman of this association. I am a secretary of this institution. I am a member of this Parliament. I am the head of this delegation. I made this discovery. I am the author of this book. I am the editor of this journal. I am the manager of this factory. I am the head of this office.

This "I-ness" is the root cause of dissension and disharmony in life. This "I-ness" is unspiritual. It is the off-shot of matter. So long as self screens and overshadows the Self — the Eternal Spirit in man, the knowledge of the Self which is so necessary in life can never be attained. We have to worship Self and not non-Self. The Gita says: "Know thou that *Prakriti* as well as *Purusha* are both beginningless; and know thou also that all forms and qualities are born of *Prakriti*." (Discourse XIII–19). Attachment to the qualities born of *Prakriti* is the cause of *samsara* i.e. so long as man is attached to forms,. has earthly desires and is not free of the ego, he can never attain liberation. The Gita says: "*Purusha,* when seated in *Prakriti,* experiences the qualities born of *Prakriti.* Attachment to the qualities is the cause of his birth in good and evil wombs."

(Discourse XIII–21.)

Man is Spirit. He has to lead the life of spirit to understand and realise the Self within him. God is Spirit. Man too is spirit. For did not Christ say: "That they all may be one, as Thou Father art in me and I in Thee, that they may also believe that Thou has sent me.

And the glory which Thou gavest me, I have given them, that they may be one, even as we are one."

(St. John Ch. XVII–21 and 22)

Unity of God is taught in all principal religions. There is no separateness of life. We all are sparks of God and we have to life for one another, as members of one World Family and not for individual enjoyment or glorification. The wrong conception that life is meant for self-enjoyment and self-maintenance should be eradicated. We have to live, not to serve our selfish interests. To serve the cause of all humanity is the object of life. To forget self in the service of others is the dictum of all religions. Did not Christ

say, "Whosoever shall seek to save his life, shall lose it; and whosoever shall lose his life shall preserve it.
(St. Luke Ch. XVII–33).

Said Christ: "These things I command you, that you love one another." (St. John Ch. XV–17). Love is the cementing link in the edifice of life. Why the great saviours and founders of religion made such great sacrifices in their lives? Because they loved God and loved all mankind and wanted to liberate man from the thraldom of pain and suffering. Zoroaster, Krishna, Buddha, Christ, Mohammad made sacrifices, so that they may help all mankind by showing to them the way of liberation.

It is said of Lord Zoroaster that he retired in the seclusion of mountains and prayed and fasted for days and nights together, so that he might attain divine knowledge for the emancipation of the world. As a result of his renunciation, he got God's revelation. The divine wisdom attained in this manner is contained in the 21 Nasks composed by Zoroaster under the direct inspiration of Ahuramazda. Unfortunately, they are no longer in existence, having been burned to ashes when Alexander the Great invaded Iran. Such was the venom and vandalism of the invading hordes of religious fanatics.

Zoroaster was a *Magi* i.e., he was a wizard in mystical knowledge. Like Christ, he healed the sick and the ailing. He had superhuman knowledge and he wielded superphysical power. He was a Raja *Yogi* of the highest type. And the main teaching of Zoroastrianism, which became the principal religion of the world, at that time was Unity of Life. Zoroaster taught that all creatures in the universe evolved and the object of human evolution was to reach God and be united with Him. He spoke of the Supreme Universal Law — the Law of Righteousness. To co-operate with this Law, to be in tune with it, is to attain immortality.

When Zoroaster prays to Ahuramazda, he asks for two boons viz., His vision and the power to converse with Him for the establishment of Zoroastrianism. What hardships, what difficulties, what tremendous opposition, he underwent, when he came out from his seclusion to preach and spread his new religion to the world, eclipsed in darkness, are matters of history. He gave the message of the realisation of the Oneness with God, as essential for man's emancipation.

Buddha also spoke of liberation, though his method of attaining *nirvana* was different. His was the teaching of quietism. Meditation formed the principal part in Buddha's teaching for seeking liberation. In Zoroastrianism, it is not seclusion, but rigid struggle in the day to day life to overcome evil and establish righteousness, which is the keynote of its teaching.

Mohammad, the founder of Islam, got revelation through Angel Gabriel by leading a life of seclusion and meditation. Islam also, like Zoroastrianism lays emphasis upon conquest of evil by leading a life of rigid activity. There is no place in Islam and Zoroastrianism for any system of monasticism, renunciation or quietism, as we find in Hinduism, Buddhism and Christianity. But it must be remembered that the founders of all religions including Islam and Zoroastrianism attained to God's revelation by a life of renunciation, seclusion, prayers and meditation. "Many are called but few are chosen." says Christ. A life of seclusion, renunciation and meditation is absolutely necessary for those who yearn to attain to the highest stage of spirituality viz., union with God. Religion is meant for the masses. The Science of the Higher Truths as embodied in Mysticism is meant for those who have entered the Path and are under the guidance of their Masters. Renunciation and meditation form the principal spokes in the wheel of Spirituality.

God is Spirit and if the objective is union with God, man must lead a spiritual life and not the life of the flesh. Things which are transient and ephemeral have no place of importance in the life of the spirit.

Oneness with God, means oneness with all. Oneness with all means love, sacrifice, peace, harmony, purity, austerity, fullness of life, leading to eternal bliss.

O God, this is our fervent prayer to Thee that Thou in Thy wisdom shalt vouchsafe to us the spirit of self-sacrifice, so that discarding the ways of the world, we by the way of the Spirit, come to Thee and be merged like a drop in The Ocean of Eternal BLISS.

O God, Thou art Eternal BLISS
How I wish Thy feet, to kiss,
In all humility and reverence
And feel Thy presence by Thy fragrance.

O God, Thou art Spirit, not matter
I seek to leave this fetter.
Which binds me to the wheel of sin,
And did adieu to this world of din.

DISCOURSE NO. XVII

The Light of Love

Says Paul Andrew: 'God never stops calling all men. He never stops calling each of us. By name and in a thousand different ways — He compels us finally to recognise the fact that God loves us. That He wishes us to share the Christian Joy and Ministry.

Often we perceive it only after a long period of time. Then with miraculous precision the facts become amazingly clear. Then we understand that such experiences are to teach us what God expects of us."

Christ's mission on earth was one of LOVE. He was full of love. Love flowed from his heart like a river, watering the deserts of life and bringing the joy of God in desolate hearts. His heart was centered in God. He knew, God loved all His children and He was the Torch-bearer of God's love to all mankind. To the humanity in wilderness, he said: "I and My Father are One." "Love God and love your neighbour and we shall all be one with God." That was the essence of his teaching, the main purpose of his mission. Except Pharisees and Sadducees, who were hostile to him and who were denounced as hypocrites, people flocked to him, as he was full of love. He taught them in parables the great truths of God.

Sinners took refuge in him. Nay, he even dined with publicans for his was the mission to win all by the magic of his heart. The sick in soul invariably got his first attention for Christ's ministry was principally meant for them. He eradicated evil by the magic of love and instilled God's light in forlorn hearts. People rushed to touch even the hem of his garment, for they knew that it would transform them. Such was their faith in Christ — the living monument of God's love to all mankind.

The simple folks — the fishermen of Galilee — were the first to follow Christ. He loved them and they loved him. They were pure in heart and Christ said: "Blessed are the pure in heart for they shall see God."

(St. Mathew Ch.V–8).

Christ's whole teaching is based on LOVE — universal love, for the child, the sinner and all alike in the whole universe. Buddha taught: "Hatred ceaseth not by hatred; hatred ceaseth by love." But Christ's teaching of love was supreme. He said: "But I say unto you which hear, Love your enemies, do good to them which hate you. Bless them that curse you and pray for them which despitefully use you.

And unto him that smiteth thee on the one check, offer also the other; and him that taketh away thy cloke, forbid not to take thy coat also." (St. Luke Ch. VI–27, 28 and 29).

How very grand and mystical is this great teaching of love and forgiveness. It is unsurpassed in the history of the world. Judge not, condemn not, be merciful, give all without calling it back, love even your enemies, do good for the sake of good, out of love, mercy and kindness, take all into your bosom, as if they were companions of your soul—this is the teaching of Christ, which reminds us of the great truths revealed by God to the *Rishis* of India in the olden days.

Christ's central teaching to his disciples was:

"Take no thought for your life, what by shall eat; neither for the body, what ye shall put on.

The life is more than meat and the body is more than raiment."

(St. Luke Ch. XII, 22 and 23).

No man can make a willing sacrifice unless he has a loving heart. It is then, he makes sacrifice, a joy in life. His constant thought is not of himself but of others. He, in fact, provides loss for himself, so that he may help others with the fullness of his heart.

But the question is whether Christs's great teaching of love finds an echo in human hearts, even in Christian countries? If so, why should there by WAR? Is there anything more monstrous and devilish than War? To draw the sword to settle disputes between a nation and a nation, to fight for territorial aggrandisement, to stain the ground with the blood of the innocent, to ruin peaceful homes and cause endless misery and suffering — is there a monster, so great as of War? Is this civilization or Christianity, if war should still stalk the land causing misery, untold suffering and ruination? We are so linked to-day, one with the other, that any war soon gives rise to a global war, and it is fought with savage fury aided by atom and hydrogen bombs, the latest devices of man's monstrosity, for wholesale human destruction.

Man-made laws, man-made political maps, man-made geographical boundaries, man-made systems of thought, have to give way for God's Law of Universal Love, Peace, Brotherhood and Harmony. It is God's Plan and design that man shall enter His Kingdom of Happiness. He never stops calling us. He loves us all. When God is all LOVE and FORGIVENESS, can we not love one another and forget and forgive every deed of iniquity and live in peaceful neighbourhood?

Unless Christ's great teaching of love is made to burn incessantly in the altar of our heart. War will still stalk the land.

This is then our prayer to Thee, God, that Thou shalt renew the spirit of Christ in each of one of us, so that we may not fail in spreading the seeds of Love and Fraternity in all the ranks of life and in all the realms of the world. May War be outlawed for all time and Peace be established throughout the world. Amen!

Peace and Brotherhood

O God, Thou sent Christ as Thy messenger of Love,
He was meek and kind and gentle as a dove.
But his message of Love, needs renewal
For man has become too cruel and carnal.

Hatred is the demon of ruination,
Pride is the monster of frustration.
Lust is the seed of destruction,
Anger bespeaks devastation.

May we cast out these germs from our mind,
And sow new seeds of another kind,
Seeds of Love and Peach and Brotherhood,
And make the world one great neighbourhood.

DISCOURSE NO. XVIII

God and His Angels

Said Kabir, "Ram and Rahim, Krishna and Karim are different names of the one Lord." There is one God who rules the universe. He is the Lord of the invisible and visible. He is the creator and controller of all things under the sky and all beings in the universe He is beginningless; He is endless. He is Omnipotent, Omnipresent, Omniscient. He is with attributes. He is without attributes.

In Avesta, He is known by the name of Ahuramazda. Ahuramazda is depicted in Zoroastrian theology both as the Invisible Creator of the universe as well as an *Amshaspenta* and even a *Yesta*. As an *Amshaspenta,* He is the head of the Seven *Amshaspenta,* and as a Yezta, He is the head of innumerable *Yeztas*. *Yeztas* may be compared to smaller gods, working under the supremacy of the Supreme Lord, who is both visible and invisible — invisible to the naked eye but visible to the inner eye of the mystic.

In Christianity, He is known as God, the Supreme Lord of creation, matchless, most adorable, most worthy of worship. He is surrounded by a number of lesser Gods —His own creation — the Principalities, the Thrones, the Cherubims, the Seraphs, the Angels and the Archangels. Each of these Celestial Beings is entrusted by God with powers to function in the Celestial Hierarchy, according to the order they belong to, for the fulfillment of God's universal Law of PEACE and HARMONY.

In Islam, God is known as *Allah*, one without an equal, supreme in the universe, to whom obeisance is to be paid by all creatures in the universe from man to the highest angel. *Allah* is one, who according to the holy Quran, is to be feared, loved, adored and worshipped, unstintedly, unreservedly, undiminishingly, with unabated breath. He is the giver and bestower of health and happiness. He is the Father of the orphan. He is the Friend of the lonely.

In Hinduism, God is known as *Brahman, Sat Chit Ananda*, Absolute Existence, consciousness, BLISS. He is both transcendent and immanent.

"I, O Gudakesa, am the Self, seated in the heart of all beings. I am the beginning, the middle and the end of all beings."

(Bhagvad Gita Ch. X–20)

Hindus believe in many *Devas*, but that does not mean to say that Hinduism is not a monotheistic religion. *Devas* are the shining ones, who may be compared to *Amshaspantas* and *Yeztas* of the Zoroastrians and Seraphs, Angels and Archangels of the Christians. The *Devas* serve under One Supreme Being and they are given authorities over certain elements only — all working co-operatively for the success of God's Plan of Evolution in the universe.

The Jews call their God — *Jehavah,* the Supreme in the universe, Matchless, all Wise, Benevolent and Merciful.

Salutations be to Thee, O Lord, and to those Celestial Beings, who guard and protect the elements who work vigilantly day and night in accordance to Thy command for the promotion of Thy Law of Universal Peace.

God alone is worthy of supreme worship. He is the Knower. He is the Deliverer. He is the Perceiver. He is the Protector. He is the ultimate basis of the universe. He is Eternal. He is Infinite. He is the Ocean of Compassion. He is the Mountain of Love. He is the Beloved of the worshipper. He is the Singer, whose sweet voice is wafted across the wide vistas of Nature and it touches silently the inner chords of the human heart. He is the incense; He is the frankincense; He is the sandalwood, the burning fragrance of which dwells in the heart, subjugates the senses and enthralls the mind for higher work in life. He is the inspirer. His holy name, sung in different ways, is the talisman against all ills. He is the Father, He is the Mother, He is the Kinsman. He is the Preceptor of all those who seek Him. He is the God of Gods. He is the Saviour. He is the Evolver. He is the Liberator. He is beyond birth, death and decay. He is Changeless. He is Indestructible. He is Sleepless. He is equipoised, He is Timeless, Beginningless, endless. He lives in the heart of every human being and lifts the human soul to the highest spiritual ecstacy. Causeless, Mightiest, He is the Supreme Lord in the universe. Who would not love Him, adore Him and worship Him?

God

O God, Thou art the Supreme Lord in the universe,
The theme of praise in prose and verse.
Invincible, Invisible, Matchless, Causeless,
Thou art the soul of the dauntless.

Beginningless, Endless, Timeless,
Thou stirreth the heart tireless,
To sing the song of love and goodness,
Is that not divine madness?

Eternal, Infinite, Unborn, Self-born,
The seed of every ear of corn,
Thou art the rose and the fragrance.
O, give us the light of Thy presence.

Thou art the Lord of all the elements,
The cure of all ailments,
The Harbinger of Peace and Rest.
The Evangelist of East and West.

Thou art the Saviour and Redeemer,
Thou art the Revealer and Forgiver.
Thou art the Source of Light,
We seek Thee, day and night.

DISCOURSE NO. XIX

Nature's Grandeur

Nature is a vast mirror of God's greatness and grandeur. The mountains that soar high, the rivers that glide and fall into the mighty ocean, the deep ravines, the murmuring brooks, the tall trees — the banian and the oak, the pine and the cocoa palm, — the still lake, the roaring sea, the sweeping wind, the rose-scented zephyr, the green meadows, the verdant fields laden with golden corn, the sylvan farms, the azure blue vault of the sky studded with stars in the silvery night — are these not the living movements of God's greatness and grandeur?

Every part of Nature speaks of God. The whole Nature is the body and God the Soul. The birds that sing in the early hours before the break of dawn, the glorious red ball of the sun, when it rises in the horizon, the freshness of the morning, when simple peasants wend their way to their farms, to plough the land and water the fields, the ringing of the church-bell, rousing people to come to the village chapel, the milk maids that saunter in the morning with cans and pails of milk and boys who go merrily on their errand rounds — do they not all awaken thoughts of serenity, bordering on God?

Nature's charm lies in its simplicity. To be natural is to be simple: it is to be God like. Every colour of the sky is the forefinger of ecstatic beauty. There is unrivalled beauty in the rose, in the rainbow, in the sky studded with silvery moon and countless stars, in the silent waters of the lake, in the setting of the sun in glorious red, like a ball of fire, illumining the sky with variegated colours, so very ravishing to the eye and refreshing to the soul.

Nature is sublime. It lifts the soul to heights of ecstasy beyond human comprehension. It is our guide our teacher, it is our inspirer. It is our consoler. It is the companion of the soul, the ravisher of the heart. It enflames the mind. It creates streams of joy, running wildly, inwardly and calls on man to think of ONE who is SUPREME in the universe.

God dwells in the human heart. He dwells in Nature. He is immanent in every being. He is transcendent and pervades the whole universe. Every petal of the rose, every tint of colour, every waft of the breeze, every leaf of the tree, every song of the bird, every swell of the sea, every drop of dew, every soul on earth, — they remind us of God's glory.

To live with Nature is to live with God. To dwell on its beauty is to commune with God. There is no music greater than of the rustling wind, the gliding river, the birds that sing and hop merrily. The silvery light of the moon and twinkling of the stars, provide a ravishing fare for the soul's ecstatic dance.

The sun is the monitor of our conscience. It is our prelate and pontiff.

Even if we do not see the Masters, who guide and help this suffering world of ours and all those angels and archangels of the celestial order, who keep an eye on us and above all. God, our Lord and Creator, the Supreme in the universe, the visible Nature in its splendour and sublimity is an enough guide and preceptor to our soul to rise to the highest pitch of spirituality.

O God, this is our earnest prayer that we may come nearer and nearer to Thee by listening to the voice of Nature and by living with Nature, become One with Thee — the Be-All and End-All of Life.

Nature

I see Thee in the green meadow.
I see Thee in every shade and shadow.
I see Thee in the smiling child.
I see Thee in the rivers that glide.

I see Thee in the leafy forage.
I see Thee in Nature's storage.
I see Thee in the sun and moon.
I see Thee everywhere, night and noon.

I see Thee in rain and sushine.
In Nature's Hall, I dine.
Nature is my preceptor.
Nature is my guide and teacher.

I love to be with Nature.
It gives me soul's culture,
I need no other inspiration,
Than Nature's school of introspection.

In all weathers and in all seasons.
Nature's guidance for all reasons,
Is the best nourisher of the soul,
Which has God for its goal.

DISCOURSE NO. XX

Religion

"Brahman is Anandam," God is Joy, transcendental BLISS, joy that knows no bounds and sweeps the soul inwardly and makes it dance in ecstatic delight. Such is God's bliss in human heart. The more of God in man, the more of life, the more of bliss, in him. This is the teaching of all religions in the world.

The centre of every religion is God. The object of religion is to tell man, that he is not alone in the universe. He is linked with the Supreme Lord and the whole of the Celestial Hierarchy. Not only God protects and guides him in his pilgrimage, but the Masters. Angels, Archangels, *Yeztas, Amshaspents*. Devas, Seraphs, Principalities — all these Celestial Beings, have their eyes on him, directly or indirectly. The Law of Harmony works in Nature and the workers of this Law are the invisible spirits, who carry out God's orders for the maintenance and welfare of the whole world. But for them the world to-day would be in ruins.

Man is spirit but the senses and the mind are the greatest impediments to the growth of the soul within him. It is to teach him how to life in life, how to avoid the pitfalls, how to escape from the snare of temptations, how to enter into the path of light and to discard things which are shadowy and ephemeral, — that is the role of religion.

Religion is the helm of the ship of life. It is the beacon light in the stormy sea of life. It is the pillar on which we fasten our hopes for the future. It is our FAITH CENTRE. It is our friend and ally. It is the greatest consoler of the soul, especially in the hour of distress.

Religion is often mistaken for a tangle of rites and rituals. Whatever notion one may have for rites and ceremonics performed in the name of religion, to look upon such observance as religion itself is absurd. They are meant as instruments to stir the soul to the higher things of life. Churches and temples, mosques and synagogues are necessary in life, especially for the masses. These Houses of God — there congregation halls, are the symbols of man's faith in God.

Whether we attune ourselves to God by performing rites and ceremonies, attending churches and temples, burning incense and sandalwood, the most important thing that is wanted to link us with God is the devotion of the heart and purity of life and self-sacrifice. God is not concerned with the arithmetic, geometry or trigonometry of prayers. Whether you offer prayers to Him in the temple or the mosque, or in the secret sanctuary of your home, what is essential is the sincerity and purity of the heart. To create true devotion to God, in whatsoever form it may be and by whatever means is the objective of religion.

The essential philosophy of religion is that man's soul is a spark of God. It enters into the human body for the purpose of gaining experiences, good or bad, pleasant or unpleasant. When the soul in the physical body is perfected, it re-units with God and its earthly peregrinations stop.

Re-incarnation is the fundamental teaching of all mystic religions, though Christian church, orthodox Islam and modern Zoroastrianism may denounce it. Re-incarnation and the Law of Karma are indisputable and indispensable factors of life and not mere vague theories.

Religion is the function of the soul. It is our lodestar. It is the ladder that takes us to God — the greatest Being in the universe. It is the bridge that covers the gulf between this world and other worlds. It is the signpost of soul's salvation. It is the light that drives away the demon of ignorance and cleanses the slums, breeding germs of disease, decay and death.

Man's aim in life is to reach immortality. His spirit has moved from Eternity and it shall live for Eternity. There is no sinner so great, as will not evolve through a cycle of births and deaths, till at last it reaches a stage of perfection, when the soul is immersed in the Ocean of God — Eternity.

They are really irreligious, who in their pretence of love for God and religion, carry their fanatic crusades against men of other faiths, on the ground that their religion is the best. All religions are pathways to God. Really speaking, there should be no need or ground for conversion. Religious intolerance, religious bigotry, religious idolatory, religious fanaticism, add to the venom of life and create frustration and disharmony. The horrors of the Inquisition in the medieval ages have still left a ghastly memory.

The object of religion is to create harmony, not disharmony, brotherhood, not hostility, love, not hatred. They are the Pharisees and Sadducees, who stick to the external observance of Law and not to the spirit to religion.

O God, this is our earnest prayer to Thee, that Thou shalt give us strength to observer the Religion of all religions — the Religion of Truth, the Religion of Righteousness, the Religion of Love, the Religion of mutual understanding, the Religion of Brotherhood in spirit and mind.

Religion

Religion is the teacher of the soul;
It shows the way to the goal,
From the glittering *maya* of the world,
To the gates of heaven unfurled.

It teaches love for God and man.
It frees us from life's den.
It is the gateway to Eternity:
It leads us from uncertainty, to certainty.

It is a ladder from darkness to light,
It is a solace in the hour of night.
It makes us fasten our heart and mind on God,
It is a gateway to the Supreme Lord.

DISCOURSE NO. XXI

Masters

Is there anything greater than religion? Can religion be transcended? Yes. It is said in the Bible, "Many are called but few are chosen." The few chosen are those who come under the direct guidance of Masters. Masters are perfected human souls, who having attained their liberation, either serve mankind in physical body or spirit body. They are called Adepts or *Jivan Muktas*. Theosophists know their Spirit Masters, as Members of the Great White Brotherhood. It is an intermediary circle which has its abode in the celestial realm but whose main function is on this earth plane. They work under the direct orders of God, who is the Master of Masters. They have tremendous powers. They can take any body they like, physical, astral, mental spiritual. They can fly in the air, walk on the waters, penetrate through dense matter. They are spirits of a very high order, evolved from the human soul. These Masters are given different portfolios for the maintenance and welfare of this world of ours.

There are two groups of Masters. One group is concerned with the welfare of the world as a whole. They work in different aspects for the amelioration of the people of the world, educationally, socially, morally, economically, politically and spiritually. All the different activities of men are as if it were dominated by the will of the Masters, working in different circles for specific purposes. Their number is large for God is Infinite and His Kingdom is infinite. Their chief work is by inspiration. They are invisible helpers serving the cause of mankind. But for them the world would go to pieces.

The second group of Masters is composed of those who contact human souls, individually and help them in attaining their liberation. Each liberated human soul is a great force and asset for the progress of the world. Individual liberation and general welfare of the world — these two form the dominant functions of the Masters. We shall now deal with the Master's work in liberating human souls.

We have already said that "Many are called, but few are chosen." Religion is meant for the masses. The Science of the Masters, is meant only for the few, chosen by God. It is therefore higher than religion and is composed of mystical teachings. Only those who have succeeded in perfecting their character to a certain extent and show an inclination for entire renunciation of the world, and whose heart and mind and soul are devoted to God, are selected by God for Master's training and they enter the Path. When once a disciple enters the stream, he has to go headlong. There is no going back. He is helped onward and onward and he pushers on till he reaches the goal.

When the disciple enters the Path, it is a signal of his entering on a new career of life. He becomes a mystic seeker of truths in life. His soul haunts for mystical training and the Master is his guide and preceptor. In order to give him mystical training and guidance the Master's first work is to perfect the soul of the disciple. He is made fearless. His egotism is crushed to pieces. His faith in God and his Master is strengthened. His desires are killed. He is purified in mind, body and soul to the highest extent. He realises that fullness of life is attained only when he lives not for himself but for others. Unity of life is the predominant lesson taught to him by the Master. He sees himself now in a different light. He sees that there is no wall of separation between him and other creatures. He becomes impersonal. He loves all without attachment. He has no hatred for any one. He is full of love, mercy, compassion. To him friend and foe are alike. Saint or sinner, makes no difference to him. His code of ethics teaches him to work without expectation of any return or reward to love all without any distinction of religion or nationality and to worship God, the Lord of the Universe and the Lord of his heart, in the secret sanctuary of his inner self with all earnestness and sincerity.

When the Master sees that his pupil has made sufficient progress, he gives him psychic powers. They are tremendous mystical powers to be gained by spiritual efforts and not by artificial means, which are often employed by foolish people to gain ascendency over others. These psychic powers help the disciple on the path, for he becomes now a mystic pilgrim. He can now talk with his Spirit Master and see his Spirit Master.

There are various stages on the path which are called Initiations in the phraseology of Theosophists. We shall not discuss these stages one by one. It takes generally seven incarnations for a human soul to finish the path and reach the goal — the goal of Adeptship. If the soul is not very keen in its efforts, it may take even seventy incarnations. But it is possible to finish the whole path even in one stride. This requirs determination on the part of the human soul. Will plays a most dominant role in the life of the disciple, when once he has entered the stream. It is a tremendous force. The dynamic will of man can break all barriers and sail successfully through all waters. To a man of will, nothing is impossible. Will is Eternity.

It is idle to discuss whether a *guru* in physical body is better than a Spirit Master in training the disciple on the path. Both equally serve the purpose. But it is our opinion, that God so arranges that He first brings the disciple for training under a physical *guru* — a *Jivan Mukta* and when the disciple has reached a certain stage of perfection, he contacts his Spirit Master who eventually takes him to the final goal.

The Bible describes the narrow path and the broad road. The narrow path which the disciple has to tread is exceedingly difficult. It is beset with many dangers. It is thorny and stony but it is the only path to attain salvation. The Master's guidance on this path is indispensable. He so trains the disciple, that he becomes indifferent to difficulties, dangers and doubts that beset him. His mind and heart and soul are so fastened on God, that earthly attractions lose their allurement and difficulties and casualties their sting. He becomes absolutely impersonal. He cares not for name or fame, wealth or riches, glory or power. All he knows is that he is a link in the chain of one vast human brotherhood. He leads a life of renunciation, prayers and meditation. Meditation is the most important fulcrum in the life of the spirit. It is meditation that can open the third, inner eye and this can be done only under the guidance and training of a Master or a Master of Masters i.e., God Himself. Usually it is the Master that takes the disciple to the goal of his life. But in rare cases, God, Himself, the Master of Masters, becomes the trainer and preceptor of the disciple, in the later stages of the Path.

The first most important stage is that of Arhatship. When the pupil becomes an Arhat, he becomes fit for *nirvana,* i.e., salvation. He need not then be re-born on this earth plane. But often, the human soul aspires to become a *Jivan Mukta* in this very round of life. This course from Arhatship to *Jivan Mukti* is exceedingly difficult. The disciple is subjected to several tests, trials and tribulations. But such is the spell of the aura of the Master, that if the disciple wills he can overcome all barriers of temptation, tests and trials, that he is exposed to.

As we have already said, souls liberated have the option to return to the earth or continue their journey on the earth plane after getting liberation before they are called away as it happened in the instances of

Buddha and Sankaracharya. Their renunciation must be considered to be of the highest type. Buddha served as we know for full forty years and more, after attaining *Nirvana*. His is classical renunciation along with that of Sankaracharya — the two greatest spiritual stalwarts that India has produced.

O God, this is our prayer to Thee, that Thou in Thy great kindness and mercy will give us the guidance of Thy Masters, to guide us on the path and to bring us, face to face, to Thee, our Lord, the Master of Masters.

Masters

I am ready for the Path, the Master is come.
Sweet words in my ear do hum.
I am ready to carry our My Master's will.
I am ready for all desires to kill.

To work under the aura of the Master,
Is to progress faster and faster.
He is the guide and the preceptor,
He is the inspirer and the benefactor.

He can free the soul from human bondage:
He can release it from world's wild rage.
The Master's love is supreme and sublime.
It is above all reason and rhyme.

It is the Master who gives the psychic gift
For the soul to rise and not to drift.

It is He who takes the soul to journey's end.
Such is God's Plan and soul's trend.

Scriptures fail, when the Master is there,
He gives us the highest spiritual fare,
He tunes the soul in diverse ways
To see God, face to face.

DISCOURSE NO. XXII

One World Government and One World Religion

The various scientific discoveries have annihilated distances of time and space and made the world a small unit. A talk given in London or any other place in the world, can be heard on the wireless, everywhere in the course of a few seconds. The radio stations hum with news all the time.

The radio has become an indispensable factor in the civilised and cultured life of the nation and the individual. Church music, beautiful songs, speeches, political and sports news, talks on educational and social problems, health reviews, economic surveys and so forth form the daily menu of the intellectual food served by the radio. The radio is the unifying instrument, as if the world was one body with one soul. It brings all in its enticing snare and spreads intellectual food for the entertainment of all. It could be the greatest harmonising factor in life. It is true, that the radio is often abused and made an instrument for broadcasting venom and hatred, when political passions are aroused.

The discovery of atom and hydrogen bombs is another factor, which brings us to mind that the world has become a small unit and can be wiped off in no time, if man's evil nature gets ascendency over other considerations.

The discovery of acroplanes has upset all ideas of distances. Our forefathers in undivided India, used to travel by bullock cart, which went at the royal speed of two or three miles an hour. The speed of an ordinary aeroplane to-day is not less than 150 miles an hour. A big air liner takes one from the Federal Capital of Pakistan to London, which once used to be the focus of the world, in the course of less than twentyfour hours a distance of more than 5000 miles.

What we mean to say is that modern scientific discoveries have brought home to us this fact of our neighbourhood to all men of the world. We no longer live in water-tight compartments, separated by barriers of long distances. There is a tremendous intercourse of people, moving from one distant place to another. The Chinese meets the Siamese, the Indonesian greets the Abyssinian, the American contacts the African, the Austrialian hails the Indian, the Russian salutes as his comrade every socialist of the world. This wide intercourse has brought to the forefront the questions of internationalism.

Having come to this conclusion, that A living in America, B in China, C in Africa, D in the Arctic Ocean, are on the level of a very intimate relationship with one another, is it not our concern to take advantage of this situation and knit all the countries of the world into one harmonious whole? The justification for coalescing different countries, with different governments, different customs, different cultures and religions, is that such a course in the very first instance would obliterate all chances of any war, which is a most monstrous engine and instrument of human degradation and destruction. We have already gone through the horrors of two world wars and people apprehend a third world war. Each country looks upon its neighbour with the eyes of suspicion and the race for armaments has not ceased.

We have made attempts to outlaw war by devising various means such as founding the United Nations Organisation, the objective of which is to settle amicably national and political differences without recourse to arms. Experiences so far gained do not coincide with expectations held out.

So long as countries are governed separately, by their own nationals, nationalism which is to-day the worst source of animosity in the world, will continue to be the spearhead of unrest and misery in the world. National aggrandisement, national greed, national rivalry, national hatred, national jealousy will continue to play their blatant part and the world's turmoil will not come to an end. The only means of controlling world's unrest caused by the venom of narrow nationalism, is by coalescing all the countries of the world and bringing them under the subjection of one world government. This will obliterate nationalism and remove the oppression of minorities in different countries.

The system of one world government, which is not an impracticable idea in view of the circumstances related, will be the greatest bulwark against war. Socrates took pride in saying that he was not a citizen of Athens, but a citizen of the world. This Socratic spirit must enter into every one of us. Nay, we should go even a step further and say, that we are not only citizens of the world but citizens of the Cosmos.

This will obliterate the necessity of different religions being followed by different people. Scholars and seers have proved to the hilt that all religions are the same in their essential teachings. Each religion has more or less the same philosophy and the same code of ethics. The only difference that exists between one religion and another is in the observance of rituals, dogmas, rites and ceremonies. There are all man-made and truly speaking they have no religious importance. It is high time all religions were coalesced into one universal religion for all mankind to follow. It will do away with religious bigotry, superstition, undue observance of rites and ceremonies and above all the arrogance of belief, by Christians, that christianity is the best religion, by Hindus, that Hinduism is the best, by Zoroastrians, that Zoroastrianism is the best and by Mohammadans, that Islam is the best religion and so forth. When the essential teachings of all religions are absolutely the same, the necessity of one world. Religion becomes all the more imperative. Such a sense of relgious unity, will remove all political and geographical barriers and gather momentum for true fellowship and brotherhood all over the world.

Establishment of one world government and one world religion, presupposes the employment of one world language. The language at present spoken the most, in the world is English. It is not our desire to enter into merits and demerits of this question. But we must make this bare statement of the fact, that English is known all over the world and as such it would be a very convenient language for One World Government.

It is our most earnest prayer to Thee, O God, that Thou shalt sent a messenger, who shall unity all the present different religions — viz., Zoroastrianism, Hinduism, Buddhism, Judaism, Christianity, Islam, Sikhism and so forth and spread the universal message of unity of life under the banner of One God, one Religion, one Race and one Language.

One World Religion

Zarthustra and Krishna, Buddha and Moses,
Christ and Mohammad, were spiritual roses.
They came to stir the hearts of people
And create in their mind a mighty ripple.

They broke the fence of folly,
And showed the way that was holy.
They taught purity in thought, word and deed,
And made men godly, indeed.

Those ancient prophets have finished their mission,
They strove and worked without remission.
We seek now another Christ, Zoroaster,
To free us from this life's fetter.

We want a Saviour for all mankind,
To worship God in universal mind.
One Church, one Religion for all
For that is now God's own call.

PART III

SPIRITUAL POEMS

(Minocher K. Spencer)

1. Soul's Growth

Life's race begins with birth of child.
The mother smothers it with kisses, wild.
The child is like Nature's flower.
Smiling so radiant in every bower.

Soon childhood swells into boyhood.
And the lad takes stride into manhood.
World's feasts and flattery please his ears;
When he is still in tender years.

He swaggers and talks of all things,
He displays his knowledge of all the kings.
But he knows little of the King of kings,
In his ear, no divine music rings.

He takes to bride a damsel fair,
Life is a dance and a joyous fare.
But all that glitters is not gold,
He realises, when the glitter loses its hold.

He soon shuns pleasures of the youth.
His heart pines for God and Truth.
The *maya* of the world, he discards in a flash.
He wants God alone and no trash.

Youth's folly he disdains,
God's memory alone he retains.
God is his Father, God is his Mother;
God is his comrade and his brother.

God's wisdom flows in him like a river.
He listens to tale of woe and wipes the orphan's tear.
He is a brother to every man in pain,
He seeks for himself, no gain.

He sees God in TRUTH and BEAUTY.
He sees God in the Bond of Unity.
Love and Harmony are Cosmic pillars;
They are soul's ravishers and thrillers.

2. God's Messenger

The room is dark, the lights are dim;
The man is sinking, the struggle is so grim.
Anxious faces flit in gloom,
They await the final doom.

"It is all over" goes the whispering word.
The pall of sadness falls unheard.
The weary wife falls prostrate
At the thought of losing her mate.

The children sob, mute with pain.
The night is dark with peltering rain.
The dark clouds thunder and they pour;
It makes their grief all the more.

In this hour of darkness and despair,
They witness a sight extremely rare.
A human form walks into the room lightly,
And sits by the dying man, quietly.

He touches his forehead and bends low,
He feels his pulse which is slow.
He prays to God and lo, what sight,
The dying man wakes and sits aright.

The healing done, he leaves the place,
Radiant with God's light and grace.
He is God's messenger, who brings light,
In sickness and sorrow, day and night.

3. The Blind Beggar

There lived in a certain village of Rome,
A blind beggar who had no home.
He begged his living by singing songs,
And prayed to God to repair wrongs.

Often his songs brought no gain,
No bread, no shelter in the rain.
Hungry and worn out, he would sleep,
And lie content in slumber deep.

Blind, but not inwardly blind,
He had love for God, of unique kind.
He saw visions in ecstatic delight.
To him, it was the happiest sight.

Divine music poured in his ears;
His eyes were full of tears,
In deep gratitude to God,
His Master, Friend and Lord.

He sang the songs of God in voice so sweet,
He blessed him who gave him bread or meat.
He blessed him also, who instead, gave him words unkind.
He loved all, without distinction of any kind.

Absorbed in God, he sang of God, the Master.
With every praise of God, his heart moved faster.
The world's scoff and scorn
Did not make him mourn.

Who would not love that beggar blind?
Who would not in him heaven's treasure find?
He is the soul of God, His radiant eye.
What if the world calls it fie.

4. Nature's Beauty

When heart is sad and depressed,
When you feel lonely and distressed.
Stir out and seek Nature's solace.
Its charm on anguished heart is faultless.

The gorgeous valleys and the silent mountains,
The lively rivers and the ravishing fountains.
The gardens that bloom with fragrant flowers.
The green meadows and beautiful bowers,

The sweet scented zephyr that passes by.
And the birds that twitter and fly.
The deer and the antelope that gambol and frisk,
The fishes that swim not without risk.

The blue vault of the sky, moonless and starless,
When the sun rises in the morn, fierce and faultless,
The moon and the silvery stars that bedeck the sky,
When night is ushered and there is no work to ply.

These are the charms which Nature provides
For the anguished soul. It never divides
The soul from the body or the mind from the soul,
But keeps it all holy, for God is the goal.

Nature is the charmer and the teacher,
The soul's greatest ravisher.
The mystic alone knows the mystic beauty,
That God and Nature are twined in fealty.

Gorgeous Nature is God's manifestation,

It is God's own revelation.
It touches man's soul and makes him glad.
He feels thrilled, with worries fled.

O, let us take a leaf from Nature's book,
There are sermons in every stone and brook.
They purify the mind, heart and soul
And take us to our God — the goal.

5. God — Life's Goal

It is the inner urge that takes us upward.
From earth to heavenward.
To realise Self is life's greatest goal;
It is the supreme quest of the soul.

Not by riches, not by gold, not by life of passion,
Not by enjoyment of the senses, but their suppression.
Can the way to the Kingdom of God be gained,
And freedom from the wheel of birth and death attained.

God is our goal; God is our target,
How can we ever, Him forget.
He is the Lord, He is the Master.
He is the Creator, He is the Saviour.

This life is a valley of delusion.
It is a desert of desolation.
Why should we give way to frustration
And make a sorry manifestation?

Unless we lift our spirit upwards,
And cast not eyes downwards,
We shall get entangled in *maya's* snare
And lose God's love and heavenly care.

God alone is the Reality.
Let us pay Him our tribute of fealty.
He alone is our Father and Protector.
Let us serve Him, our Heavenly Father.

To love God is to love all.
To love all is to hear God's call.
We hear Him in Nature's voice,
He is our soul's supreme choice.

6. The Martyr

"To God alone belongs the entire domain"
Said the martyr, in suffering and in pain.
They whipped him and bound him to the post;
They whipped him, till blood trickled and he looked a ghost.

He bore his gnashing wounds and torment,
Without a word of fear or lament.
For to him, God was all in all,
He cared for nothing, except God's call.

His love for God transcended all the ills.
His faith in the Master rose above all the frills.
For God and Christ, he was willing to brave,
All hardships and no earthly favours, crave.

They tempted him with clothes of gold,
Rich wines and pleasures untold,
If he would leave off his madness for treasures in heaven,
And lead a worldly life and be not a craven.

To those ancient Romans, who crucified the Nazarene,
Christ's teachings were a hellish mine.
They killed Christ but not the spirit of the Nazarene,
Which shall ever endure through life's dust and din.

7. The Mystic

Here goes the silent mystic, absorbed in God;
He has no thought of self, except the great Lord.
He follows his divine Master at every step,
For earthly things, he cares not a rap.

He is humble and wise, gentle and meek,
Lean in body, he looks very weak.
But there is fire in his eye, in his checks, a red glow,
When he speaks, words of wisdom flow.

He shuns the lime light, but he is eager to share
His wonderful wisdom with those who care.
He looks upon all, the sinner and saint
As if they were same without any taint.

He heals the sick in body and in soul.
His mission is to take every one to the goal.
God is the goal, God is the light,
He gives to every one this inner sight.

Christlike, he walks with the poor and the lame.
They flock to him, every man and dame.
They love him for his face is full of divinity;
There is strength in his deep serenity.

God-like, he works for the good of all.
Strong or weak, tame or small.
He waits not to ponder or to think,
He embraces them all and does not shrink.

8. We want Brotherhood not War

War is an engine of destruction,
A holocaust of lives and ruination.
It is the cause of utter frustration,
Deep devastation, beyond human comprehension.

War is a calamity of unsurpassed nature,
In its fiendishness and bloodstained texture.
Peaceful homes are desecrated,
Trade and arts are devastated.

Man becomes a machine, a brute,
His soul is soaked in smoke and soot.
Unlimited in its monstrosity,
War is the worst atrocity.

O God, we pray to Thee with all the heart's fire,
To save us from this calamity, so dire.
We want peace, not vandalism;
We want brotherhood, not brutalism.

9. Reincarnation

Man is made of Spirit, soul and body,
Life is earnest and not a parody.
God is Spirit, dwelling in the soul of man.
Man is the maker of destiny, as beat as he can.

Spirit is the sire of the soul, a silent witness,
Mind is the apparatus of the soul, in fitness.
It is the transmitter of the internal to the external,
Likewise, in reverse order, of the external to the internal.

The influence of God in man acts upon the soul,
The influence of soul on mind, hastens access to the goal.
Rich or poor, wise or unwise.
It is the law of God, that each must rise.

Man's soul is the immortal spark of God.
It has come from God, it must return to God.
It seeks experiences through many human incarnations,
It grows wiser and wiser by lacerations.

The Law of *Karma* is indispensable,
It is God's Truth, undeniable.
As you sow, so must you reap.
Is a teaching, both mystical and deep.

There is no sinner, who can not reach salvation,
But he takes a longer time in the ladder of evolution.
Let us have spiritual feasts, not earthly pleasure,
For that leads to God in the shortest way and measure.

10. Cycle of Births

We jump from birth to birth, in *Karmic* chain.
Life is a drain and a strain.
But fearless and dauntless, we must proceed,
Through the path of thorns, to get ourselves freed.

It is *maya's* chain that keeps us tied.
Let us make God, our guide.
To free us from *maya's* snare.
And this world's glamour and glare.

God is the goal of life, not any earthly illusion,
God is the target of life, not any earthly fruition.
Let us rid ourselves from the thraldom of sin and sorrow,
By sowing seeds of righteousness, to-day, not tomorrow.

Let us forget the past and live fully
In spirit, not flesh, happily, merrily.
Not matter, but spirit is the essence;
Not sin but virtue is the frankincense.

Let us mould our destiny with God's light;
Let us develop earnestly the inner sight.
Let us treasure God's love in our mind,
And serve Him and all mankind.

Let us break the chain of *Karmic* debts,
And free ourselves from the cycle of births and deaths,
By devotion to God, in purity of mind,
By deeds of mercy to all mankind.

11. Fire

Fire, Thou art the sacred symbol of the Supreme in the universe.
In whom, every soul wishes to immerse.
To worship Thee, is to worship God,
Who is present in every seed and sod.

Thou art the miracle worker,
The greatest element in Nature.
Thou art spoken of in every Scripture.
Man adores Thee with heart's rapture.

Thou art the extinguisher of the dross,
The destroyer of the unholy and the gross.
Thou art the attire of godliness.
Thou art the symbol of righteousness.

O, let us ignite our heart, mind and soul
With the fire of mystic thoughts and reach the goal.
The hidden spark which burns, inwardly,
Must take us to God, our goal, assuredly.

12. The Lame Leper

Is there a more tragic sight,
Than of a leper struggling in his fight,
Against the inroad of the fell disease,
Which fills his body with sores, without decrease.

Forlorn, forsaken, heartlessly,
He wends his way, cheerlessly,
A spectre of human woe and suffering,
It is a sight so heart-rending.

Vanquished and exhausted he drags on.
In the chess-board of life, he is but a pawn,
Pierced by the arrows of dire misfortune.
There is note to cheer him, morn or noon.

To Christ, the leper was his brother;
He healed him without a shudder.
He saved him from life's morass,
He cured his sores and distress.

Let us Christlike befriend the leper,
And all assistance render.
He is a link in God's evolution,
A child of His creation.

13. The World is My Home

The sky is my roof, the world is my home,
From Pole to Pole, I like to roam.
To me all are brothers and sisters,
God's children, whom He ministers.

The stars are my guides,
I love star-lit rides.
In the stillness of the night,
Is not God alone the light?

The beggar and the lame, the sick and the ailing,
And all those wailing and grovelling,
Whether they be far or near,
To me are ever so dear.

They are the limbs of my body,
I am linked with every body.
Human suffering is my guide,
No secrets from my God, I hide.

May I share my joy and sorrow.
With everyone from Chilly to Cairo.
The whole wide world is my home,
From country to country, I roam.

I love all, white or brown,
As I move up and down.
The same spirit dwells in all.
Is not God, all in all ?

God is the fibre that keeps together,
Let us to Him surrender.
Humanity is one great family.
Let us live in God happily.

Is not man a microcosm,
And life a humanism ?
The loving tie, the sacred link.
Let no distance cut or shrink.

14. Full Life

Whether rich or poor, lead a life of fullness,
Free of sensuous pleasures and grossness.
There is divinity in simplicity;
There is purity in humility.

A life of spirit is a ladder of joy,
A life of flesh is a broken toy.
Speak the truth and shame the devil,
Hammer noble deeds on spirit's anvil.

A friendly word, a hearty greeting.
A radiant smile, a good hand-shaking,
Awaken the heart with warmth and freshness;
There is no tonic like frankness.

Like in thoughts of God, in fullness of heart,
Leave off the ways of the world, that are smart.
Take to the primrose path of Nature,
For, that is the best indenture.

Truth and Love make the best ingredients;
Seek not for any remnants.
To work for others is not toil,
It is pure bliss, without foil.

When the sky is studded with silvery stars,
And the moon shines along with Mars,
In that happy stillness of the night,
Is not God, in full sight?

Let us make Him, our Master and Guide,
In the panorama of life and ride,
Joyously and merrily, happily and freely,
Till we reach the goal, fearlessly.

15. God-realisation

Behold the *sanyasin*, squatting on the bank.
Free of worldly worries, above all rank.
Entranced in mystic silence, he sits,
By the running river, where none meets.

In that serene solitude of the silvery night,
He meditates and his soul takes flight,
From his body, to the highest spiritual region,
Where He meets God and His angels, in legion.

His aura is spotlessly white.
Even to angels, it is a rare sight.
Is he another Christ, who has reached that state,
With God as his Father and mate ?

There is boundless serenity in his face,
He is filled entirely with God's grace.
The inward joy, he can hardly express,
He is free of life's storm and stress.

He communes with God, day and night;
He sees the heavens, with his inner sight.
The secrets of the *Atma* are open to him like a book,
He knows God's abode and every nook.

A God-realized soul is a beacon light,
To struggling humanity in its fight,
On this earth, to attain to salvation,
The highest step in human evolution.

O God, make me a Buddha, a Christ,
Not earth, but heaven, shall be my tryst.
Let me work in spirit, to deserve Thy grace,
And meet Thee, freely face to face.

16. Forget not the Goal

I have come in trailing clouds of Beauty,
From distant past, to do my duty,
On this earth plane and go back to God,
The Creator of every seed and sod.

God is my Abode, God is my Home,
Wherever I go, wherever I roam,
I shall not forget the goal of my life,
To free myself from stress and strife.

Serenity is my watchword, Faith is my Guide,
Whether I crawl or walk, sit or ride.
It is the soul's voice, I want to hear,
Not the din of the world, but the spirit's cheer.

Forget not the goal, says the soul,
Not silver and gold, but Gold is the goal.
Not any niche in the Temple of Fame.
Nothing shall beguile me in life's game.

I shall go by the way of the Scriptures,
They are my friends, guides and teachers.
Let me ponder on their teaching,
They are my jewels, rich and ravishing.

They fire the spirit, they touch the soul,
They make me play the spirit's role.
Faith is the lamp, that can not be extinguished,
With faith in my heart, I can never be vanquished.

Courage and cheer are my youthful comparisons,
Truth and Love are my life's bastions.
When I am fortified with spirit's stronghold,
Life is a blossom, not a stranglehold.

Even worn and weary, I shall not forget the goal,
God alone is the solace of my soul.
I see Him in every nook and corner,
I see Him in every brook and border.

He is the life's star, how can I forget Him?
He is the soul's fire, how can life be dim?
He is the anchor of my heart and mind.
The link that binds me to all mankind.

17. The Storm at Sea

In the quietness of the night, rolls on the Liner,
Flooded with lights, no sight is so finer,
Than of the huge leviathan spanning the ocean,
Majestically and freely, without commotion .

There is gaiety everywhere, on the deck and in the air,
Wine flows fast and damsels are fair.
The young and old mingle, gaily and freely.
Men and women dance to music, so merrily.

There is exuberance of mirth and laughter.
Smiling faces and voices sweeter and softer,
Tingle in that vast panorama of gaiety;
In that arena of merriment, there is no satiety.

They laugh, they eat, they drink,
They dance in merriment, and not shrink.
Is not life a round of pleasures,
Why then seek distant heavenly treasures?

But lo, in the midst of that mad frivolous gaiety,
When pleasure is at its height, and in full satiety,
There goes the whispering word, that all is not well,
A storm may soon burst, who can foretell ?

The wind sweeps and gains momentum in velocity,
The clouds thunder in all their ferocity,
The ship is caught in stormy weather,
Hearts sink and they pray for shelter.

The ship is torn by stormy blasts,

The cracking timber and the masts
Topple down with heavy weight;
The engines stop, the ship meets her fate.

The weak and the strong, the frail and the brave,
They all meet their watery grave.
When God wills, how very puny is man;
He yields to death in a minute's span.

18. What Boon, I Seek

I seek no name or fame, wealth or riches,
I seek that which the soul, enriches.
Spiritual lore is greater than worldly knowledge ;
Life without spirit loses its fibre and foliage.

I ask for no land or cattle,
Earthly possessions are chaff and chattel.
Christ said: "Provide no gold, no silver."
If you wish the journey to be ended quicker.

I ask for no boon of sons and daughters,
I ask for no tall roofs or quarters.
The earth is my bed, the sky is my canopy,
With Thee, in my heart, am I not happy?

Christ came to give us the living water,
Is there any thing better and sweeter,
Than God's own spirit in us all,
Backing us to listen to His call ?

Is there any thing greater than God's name?
Earthly possessions are a shame.
They fritter our energy and keep us enslaved,
They ruin the soul and keep us encaged.

Nations fight for a mere strip of land;
Such is their lust for a sheer bag of sand,
They know not, what havoc they do.
If they sow seeds of evil, they must rue.

Nature is my bride, God is my Father,
The whole humanity is my brother.
What more boon can I want,
When He has supplied me with every want.

19. Bliss

"*Brahman is Anandam.*" God is Bliss.
Who would not like to fall at His feet and kiss ?
He is JOY and Source of Delight.
Nature is the mirror of His divine sight.

God wants all to be happy and joyful.
God wants all to lead a life that is soulful.
For, Bliss is Spirit and Spirit is Bliss,
Who would such divine joy miss?

This Bliss is in graded form.
The Law of JOY rules in every norm.
When the Sun shines, it is full of bliss;
The moon in the sky, gives silvery kiss.

There is Joy in Nature, for it is God's expression;
There is Joy in retrospection;
There is Joy in doing acts of righteousness;
There is Joy in speaking words of truthfulness.

There is Joy in communion with God in silence;
There is Joy of every king in human parlance;
The more the Bliss, the more the life;
The more the Bliss, the less the strife.

Bliss in Nature, is of the graded type,
Reaching its peak, when man is ripe,
To meet his God, face to face,
In ecstatic delight, by His grace.

Just as a mother loves her child,
Whether it is wild or mild,
She pours her love abundantly,
She gives her best delightfully.

Man should love all men, good or wicked,
For the whole pattern of life is sacred.
And this is the highest Bliss in the ladder of evolution,
For, such is the Law of God's creation.

20. Christ in Slums

Who is that white robed tall man with sunny face,
And eyes so serene, talking of God and His grace,
In that slime built slum, where the poorest stay,
In stench and darkness, without sun's ray ?

It is Christ the Saviour, the Friend of the poor,
Who emits light in darkness in his tour
Through the dark alleys and houses of the poor,
Giving messages of hope and cheer, to make them pure.

Those skinny hands, those bony cheeks,
Speak their sad tale. Are they Nature's freaks ?
No, they are the victims of man's lusts and greed,
Struggling hard for existence, from want not freed.

They live in dens of dirt and foulness,
Dressed in rags, steeped in sadness.
Gnawing poverty drives them to sin,
They lead a tragic life in that hellish din.

Sick in body, sick in soul,
Battered and blasted, they have no goal.
They drag on in woe, want and sorrow,
From day to day, from morn to tomorrow.

But lo, there comes, Christ, the Saviour,
They flock to him with hearts never so heavier.
He speaks to them the healing words of love.
He is so kind and gentle, like a dove.

He opens to them the treasure of the heavens,
Every heart, with hope, he gladdens,
He redeems the sinner and shows him the way,
The joy of suffering for that happy, final day.

21. Salvation

A life of desires is a life of pain.
He is heedless, who seeks to attain
Freedom of soul, through *mays's* glittering chain.
It is a life wasted and inane.

Mind is the parent of all desires.
Mental control is the teaching of the Scriptures.
Love for pelf and power, name and fame,
Can not enrich the soul of any·man or dame.

To train the mind by the spirit's flash.
And save it from seeking earthly trash,
Is the teaching of God to us all,
If we wish for soul's salvation and not fall.

Sow the seeds of righteousness,
Speak the words of truthfulness,
Slay the senses and the mind,
Love God and all mankind.

There is wisdom in humility.
Seek serenity in simplicity,
Soul's feast is sincerity.
Selflessness is divinity.

Self-forgetfulness, self-effacenemt
Is the Law of God's fulfilment.
To work for all without expectation of reward
Is the surest way to Salvation's award.

O God, teach us the ways of renunciation,
To attain soul's emancipation
Annihilation of the mind is the culmination
Of life's highest achievement and glorification.

22. Salutations be to Thee, O God

When I see the blue vault of the sky studded with silvery stars,
And the moon shining along with Jupiter, Venus and Mars,
An immense thrill of delight seizes my soul,
For I see God, in the moon-lit sky, — my life's goal.
Salutations be to Thee, O God.

When I see a righteous man, full of mercy and compassion,
I feel a thrill of joy and my soul is in commotion.
Righteousness is God's Law of Eternity.
It is the flagstaff of soul's fraternity.
Salutaions be to Thee, O God.

Said Christ : "Love God and all mankind."
He was gentle as a dove, so loving and kind.
He even dined with harlots and sinners,
For was not his mission to redeem transgressors ?
Salutations be to Thee, O God.

When I see a blind fakir in the street, singing a song,
Undaunted and fearless of world's wrong,
My heart goes pit-a-pat and my head bends down,
I care not for throng in the town that frown.
Salutations be to Thee, O God.

When I see a man in death's struggle,
And all gloom around the muddle,
My heart goes out to that great Creator,
To shower mercy, for He is a great radiator.
Salutations be to Thee, O God.

When I see a *yogi* near the sea-shore,
Saying his *mantras*, ever so more,
Wrapped up in thoughts of serenity,
I feel God's divinity.
Salutations be to Thee, O God.

I see God in every bush and flower.
I see God in every turret and tower.
I see God in every man and dame
Whether poor or rich, wild or tame.
Salutations be to Thee, O God.

I see God in Nature's smiling face.
I see God in every human race.
I see God in every man, kind or unkind .
The divine spark shines in every kind.
Salutations be to Thee, O God.

23. Nature's Song

The murmuring breeze as it sweeps along,
The running brook and the motley throng.
The twinkling stars and the silvery moon,
All sing of God in divine tune.

The weary sea and its melancholy,
The waves that spend themselves petulantly,
As they dash themselves against the stony shore,
Is it not divine music, more and more ?

The birds that twitter and hop from tree to tree,
So gaily and happily and so free,
The flowers that bloom by the side of the meadow,
Their sight is a song, without a shadow.

The Church bells ring in the early morn;
The fields are ripe with golden corn.
The peasants plough their land, so happily,
As they sink along, cheerfully and merrily.

The whole Nature is so kind and gay,
It opens its treasures every day.
The leafy bowers and the fragrant flowers,
Are diadems of joy, which Nature showers.

Let us dance in Nature's ecstatic joy,
And care not for any worldly toy.
For Nature is the singer of divine song.
It keeps us away from earthly throng.

Sing the song of Nature and be free,
There is God in every plant and tree.
There is God in Nature's Voice and Silence
There is God in every kind of parlance.

24. Crucifixion of Christ

Crucifixion of Christ is man's worst record of infamy.
He came as their friend, they treated him as their enemy.
He came to bless and heal both body and soul.
He came to show them the Way, the Truth, Life's goal.

But the scribes and priests of the Temple
Refused to hear him or assemble;
Christ exposed their false profession;
He denounced their retrogression.

He spoke the words of God, His Father,
To every one, he was a brother.
He loved the poor and healed the ailing.
He heard the sick and the wailing.

He was a pillar of strength to the poor,
They loved him and followed him all the more.
He mitigated their wounds and woes.
He saved them from their foes.

But such is man's lust for power and pelf,
That those who worshipped their own "self"
Shouted down Christ as a blasphemer
And spoke words of fury against this great redeemer.

They intrigued and sought the help of Roman swords,
Those degraded, heathenish hordes.
They made jesting Pilate their friend,
To serve their own nefarious end.

Christ paid the price of his holiness,
By his martyrdom to their vileness.
They lashed him till the blood trickled
And he looked sick and sickled.

They bound him down to a heavy cross,
They put on his head a crown of thorny moss,
They jestingly called him, the King of Jews,
And gave him cuts and rues.

They crucified Christ and he suffered greatest pain,
So that man may be redeemed of sin and gain
Soul's sovereignty in the realm of heaven.
Such was his sacrifice for every man and heathen.

* * *

